Thomas Cook

HOTSPOTS
BULGARIA
BLACK SEA RESORTS

Written by Debbie Stowe
Original photography by Debbie Stowe
Front cover photography by Schmid Reinhard/4Corners Images
Series design based on an original concept by Studio 183 Limited

Produced by Cambridge Publishing Management Limited
Project Editor: Penny Isaac
Layout: Paul Queripel
Maps: PC Graphics

Published by Thomas Cook Publishing
A division of Thomas Cook Tour Operations Limited
Company Registration No. 1450464 England
PO Box 227, Unit 18, Coningsby Road
Peterborough PE3 8SB, United Kingdom
email: books@thomascook.com
www.thomascookpublishing.com
+ 44 (0) 1733 416477

ISBN: 978-1-84157-758-6

First edition © 2007 Thomas Cook Publishing
Text © 2007 Thomas Cook Publishing
Maps © 2007 Thomas Cook Publishing
Project Editor: Diane Ashmore
Production/DTP Editor: Steven Collins

Printed and bound in Spain by GraphyCems

CONTENTS

WHAT'S IN YOUR GUIDEBOOK?

Independent authors Impartial up-to-date information from our travel experts who meticulously source local knowledge.

Experience Thomas Cook's 165 years in the travel industry and guidebook publishing enriches every word with expertise you can trust.

Travel know-how Contributions by thousands of staff around the globe, each one living and breathing travel.

Editors Travel-publishing professionals, pulling everything together to craft a perfect blend of words, pictures, maps and design.

You, the traveller We deliver a practical, no-nonsense approach to information, geared to how you really use it.

● *The Cathedral of the Holy Assumption in Varna*

INTRODUCTION
Getting to know the Black Sea resorts

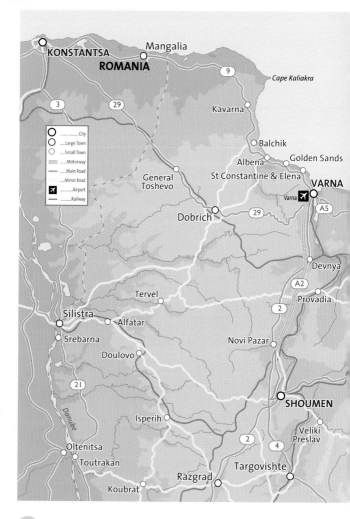

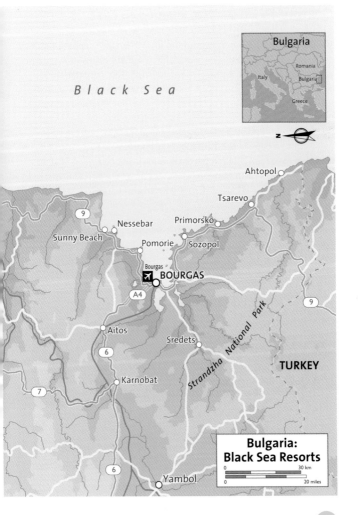

Black Sea

Bulgaria

Romania

Italy

Bulgaria

Greece

Ahtopol

Tsarevo

Nessebar

Primorsko

Sunny Beach

Pomorie

Sozopol

Bourgas

BOURGAS

A4

Aitos

Sredets

TURKEY

Karnobat

Strandzha National Park

Yambol

**Bulgaria:
Black Sea Resorts**

0   30 km

0   20 miles

Getting to know the Black Sea resorts

The Black Sea is three hours or less from most of Europe's capitals, and its golden sands, warm shallow waters, hot summer sunshine and great value prices have made it a favourite of holidaymakers since the late 1970s. Bulgaria is a Balkan nation, and offering fine hospitality is second nature here, alongside a love of street commerce, fine wine and simple but tasty food.

To all intents and purposes Bulgaria's Black Sea coast is made up of two enormous bays. Two distinct groups of resorts sit in each, satellites almost of two major cities on the coast: Varna in the north, and Bourgas

● *Flying high at Sunny Beach*

in the south. In between, fishing villages 2,000 years old provide quiet respite from the party atmosphere of the larger resorts.

Heading northwards from Varna, the bay arcs round, via the Golden Sands resort, to Cape Kaliakra. The contrast perfectly sums up the variety of the coast. Leave Golden Sands – a purpose-built temple to pleasure, chock-full of hotels, restaurants offering full English breakfasts and beach activities – then drive for one hour: you'll find yourself on a remote, windy clifftop that seems to have changed little from the Middle Ages, from where you can occasionally spot dolphins in the sea far below.

When large numbers of foreign visitors first began arriving on Bulgaria's beaches at the end of the 1970s, many could have been forgiven for thinking that life under Communism wasn't all that bad. Warm waters lapped the golden sands of the Black Sea shore, hot sunny weather, friendly locals, and gallons of cheap, excellent wine made holidays here memorable. Bulgaria's Communists, though harshly authoritarian, never managed to quell the Balkan instinct for trade and commerce, hospitality and making money. That is one reason that Bulgaria never suffered the shortages and deprivations that hit neighbouring Romania.

When the changes of 1989 swept the Communists away, Bulgaria was already established as a favourite summer holiday destination. It has since become the third most popular summer holiday destination for Britons, beaten only by France and Spain. Indeed, many holidaymakers love the place so much that they are buying second homes here.

Bulgaria has embraced this foreign invasion and the tourism industry has responded with enthusiasm to visitors' wishes and needs. While peaceful villages and quiet beaches await those who want to get away from it all, the larger resorts provide every home comfort, from Tetley tea to tabloid newspapers. Local sensitivities have adapted to Western ways and every foreign taste – be it topless sunbathing or a fry-up – is catered for.

THE BEST OF THE BLACK SEA RESORTS

Though it may not be the first place you think of for holidays by the sea, Bulgaria's Black Sea coast ticks all the right boxes. Whether you want watersports or nightlife, picturesque seaside villages, beautiful wildernesses or tradition and culture, you'll find it here.

TOP 10 ATTRACTIONS

- **Seafood at Nessebar** It may look as if there are more seafood restaurants at Nessebar than people to fill them, but prices are cheap and quality high. Everything will be fresh from the sea that day (see page 47).

- **Pomorie** Quieter and more secluded than Nessebar, Pomorie is the centre of Bulgaria's mud treatment industry; all of the village's hotels offer treatments (see page 52).

- **Varna's Cathedral** Majestic in every way from its monolithic size to its golden decoration, Varna's Cathedral of 1886 is guaranteed to take the breath away (see page 35).

- **Beach at Golden Sands** Golden Sands – a literal translation of the Bulgarian name Zlatni Pyusnati – is not the invention of an optimistic marketing man's imagination: the sand here really is as gold as you could possibly wish for (see page 22).

- **Queen Marie's Palace at Balchik** Romania's Queen Marie (who was English; a granddaughter of Queen Victoria) built a superb, Oriental-style palace here in the early 20th century (see pages 15–16).

- **Storks on the Bourgas Lakes** Twitchers are in for a treat in Bulgaria: a wonderful array of birds can be found in the marshes and lakes of Bourgas, a unique and carefully protected ecosystem (see page 86).

- **Cliffs at Kaliakra Nature Reserve** Another birdwatcher's paradise, this time with plenty for non-twitchers too. The shoreline here is steep, beautiful, remote and heavily protected (see page 66).

- **Concerts at Sozopol's Amphitheatre** Recreate the atmosphere of Roman Apollonia at the Folk Music Festival, held every summer in the peninsula's amphitheatre. The sea provides the perfect dramatic backdrop (see page 54).

- **Nightlife** Golden Sands and Sunny Beach are the Black Sea's leading nightlife destinations. Clubbers will have no trouble finding places in which to dance until dawn (see pages 27 and 45).

- **Watersports at Albena** Relatively low petrol prices make powered watersports cheap in Bulgaria, and Albena is the place for every kind of water-based fun (see page 18).

▽ *The Botanical Gardens at beautiful Balchik*

SYMBOLS KEY

The following symbols are used throughout this book:

ⓐ address ☎ telephone 📠 fax ⓦ website address ⓔ email
🕐 opening times Ⓝ public transport connections ❶ important

The following symbols are used on the maps:

𝒊	information office	○	city
✉	post office	○	large town
▣	shopping	○	small town
✈	airport	▪	poi (point of interest)
✚	hospital	═	motorway
🛡	police station	━	main road
🚌	bus station	─	minor road
🚆	railway station	—	railway
✝	church		

❶ numbers denote featured cafés, restaurants & evening venues

RESTAURANT CATEGORIES

The symbol after the name of each restaurant listed in this guide indicates the price of a typical three-course meal without drinks for one person:

£ under L12   ££ L12–L24   £££ over L24

▶ *The quayside at Nessebar*

RESORTS
Places under the sun

Balchik

Queen Marie of Romania adored Balchik. On more than one occasion she described it as her favourite place in Romania: the fact that it was in Romania at all betrays the troubled history of the region. Returned to Bulgaria in 1940 (it had been annexed by Romania after the Second Balkan War), the town is most famous as the site of the **Royal Palace**, built by the queen in the 1920s and 1930s, which sits in some splendid **Botanical Gardens**.

Today, Balchik is at peace. Rustic villas with terracotta roofs nestle among the trees on the hillside overlooking the sea, in a scene that could be straight from a turn-of-the-century painting. Perhaps because of its location at the tip of the main strip of resorts that stretch northwards from Varna, it is not such an established stop on the tourist trail as some other places, and consequently has retained a certain authenticity and unspoiled charm. Narrow cobbled streets wind sharply upwards – and are just as likely to take you to an isolated field as a smart restaurant. Take a relaxing walk and you will notice something missing from the typical seaside resort: noise. The hustle and bustle of holidaymakers is replaced by the sound of the sea breeze or an occasional bird.

This is not to say that hoteliers and restaurateurs have neglected Balchik. On the contrary, the town has some of the finest hotels in the area, almost all of which are minutes from the sea, if not on the seafront itself, and the relative quietness of the resort keeps prices reasonable. The rural atmosphere might not suggest it, but Balchik has its fair share of culture too. This makes it a good choice for anyone who wants to spend a few days getting away from the crowds without breaking the bank.

BEACHES

The general absence of hordes of tourists means that you won't have to fight for a spot on the sand in Balchik. The zoom of high-octane watersports is replaced by the distant chug of fishing boats as they pootle back and forth. From the beach you'll also have a view of the fishermen trying their luck out on the small jetties.

Indeed, this place is more about fishing than sun-worshipping, and attracts those after a bit of privacy and calm.

THINGS TO SEE & DO

Botaniceski Gradina (Botanical Gardens)

Charming though the palace is, it is almost outshone by the Botanical Gardens that surround it. In contrast to the ruggedness of the town, here nature is neat and well tended, with flowerbed after flowerbed blooming with red, yellow, white and purple. Gentle streams babble along, cottages are hidden among the trees, while a gushing waterfall provides a brief glimpse of nature untamed.

The gardens total 6.5 hectares (16 acres), and it is quite easy to get lost along the leaf-covered walkways or down the steps carved out of the hillside. It's equally easy to while away several hours just pottering around and discovering new sections. Benches are tucked away in hedges, which afford you some privacy as you sit and take in the scenery while recovering from the walking and climbing you'll have been doing.

📞 0579 76854 ✉ office@dvoreca.com 🕐 08.30–18.00
❗ Admission charge, which includes the Royal Palace

Dvoreca (Royal Palace)

By far Balchik's biggest crowd-puller is Queen Marie's palace. Owned by an English-born descendant of Queen Victoria, the palace betrays a typical English gentility. Unlike some of the garish Communist-era constructions that sprang up elsewhere in the region, the palace is understated, bearing more resemblance to a country villa than a royal seat, despite the minaret rising up from the roof that gives a nod to Islamic culture. Queen Marie would certainly have enjoyed the view from her residence, which looks straight out to sea and the cliffs further along the strip of coast.

0579 76854 office@dvoreca.com 08.30–18.00
Admission charge, which includes entrance to the Botanical Gardens

The exotic lines of Balchik's Royal Palace

Etnografski Muzei (Ethnographic Museum)

Opposite the Municipal Historical Museum is this place, which exhibits traditional Bulgarian costumes and mock-ups of homes.

ⓐ Ul Vitosha 3 ⓣ 0579 2177 ⓛ 09.00–12.00 & 12.30–16.00 Mon–Fri, closed Sat & Sun ⓘ Admission charge

Izkustvo Galeria (Art Gallery)

The Art Gallery hosts a small display of religious icons from the area, but it's worth the visit as much for the view from outside. Standing on the terrace in front of the large white building, you look out over a delightful yellow church and its bell tower. Behind is the sea, where trawlers crisscross your view.

ⓐ Ul Otets Paissii 4 ⓣ 0579 4130 ⓛ 09.00–12.00 & 13.00–16.00, Mon–Fri, closed Sat & Sun ⓘ Admission charge

Obshinski Istoria Muzei (Municipal Historical Museum)

A short walk away from the Art Gallery is the Municipal Historical Museum, which displays mostly statues.

ⓐ Pl Nezavisimost 1 ⓣ 0579 2177 ⓛ 09.00–12.00 & 12.30–16.00 Mon–Fri, closed Sat & Sun ⓘ Admission charge

AFTER DARK

Restaurants

Two Roosters Hotel and Restaurant ££ Beachfront restaurant with a large terrace and the fish specials that you would expect from somewhere so well situated. ⓐ Ul Samara 3 ⓣ 0579 76465 ⓛ 09.00–24.00

Valeo Hotel and Restaurant ££ Fine dining in a restaurant-bar that looks more like one of New York's trendiest new hangouts than a Bulgarian seaside eatery. ⓐ Ul Samara 6 ⓣ 0579 77029 ⓦ www.hotelvaleo.com ⓔ hotelvaleo@abv.bg

Albena

Exclusive, fashionable and overtly chic, Albena is as well equipped and efficient as Bulgarian coastal resorts come. One significant section of its clientele is German package tourists. Neither they nor the wealthy locals will put up with the vagaries of typical Eastern European organisation, and consequently things run smoothly.

A distinct architectural style also sets the town apart from its peers. Eschewing the tall, straight Communist-style structures that are typical of Bulgaria's hotels, many of Albena's guests lodge in pyramid-shaped hotels, reputedly designed for the rooms to have better light, and these buildings are among the most distinctive on the Black Sea coast.

It's not the cheapest of the resorts in the area, particularly for the food and drink, and you have to pay a small fee to drive into the town. But costs are still some way below what you would expect to pay in an equivalent Western European retreat. What's more, the higher prices mean that Albena is not as overrun by tourists and is therefore not as built up as some of its neighbouring resorts.

Nor is it clogged with traffic. Much of the town is pedestrianised and pleasantly verdant, and the few roads that run through it are quiet and tree-lined. You are well advised to abandon your car and take in the sights on foot or, better yet, hop on one of the little blue trains on wheels that wind around the town. Don't bother looking for road names: it's a purpose-built resort and there are none.

Children are well catered for with an array of activities from donkey rides to mini-golf and buggy racing. Adults' needs are also met. The hotels are fully 21st century and accept credit cards; many of them even have WiFi internet access for those who just can't be out of the loop. Adrenalin junkies can try parasailing or other watersports, while the lazy can simply soak up the sun or relax with a spa treatment.

There are no sites of historical interest to look around. Albena was wholly created over the past few decades with the tourist in mind. It's hedonism and holidaymaking, not history, that are what this resort is all about. More information is available at Ⓦ www.albena.com

BEACHES

Thanks to Albena's exclusivity, its beach area is less cluttered than some of the coastline further up or down. It is possible to lie on the wide, white beach with the sea in front of you, the blue sky above and only trees behind, with no sign of the tourist shops to be found elsewhere.

The beach is dotted with straw umbrellas for when the heat gets too much. But there is far more than sunbathing on offer. The beach boasts a small football pitch with two decent-sized goals, a volleyball net and some climbing frames for kids. Indeed, it's a good choice for families all round: it's upmarket, safe and clean, and the sea remains shallow for some way out, making it suitable for children's swimming.

THINGS TO SEE & DO

Excursions

Whether it's wine tasting, witnessing a mock wedding, dining at a folk restaurant or heading off in a Jeep to explore the area and visit a traditional village, Albena provides a starting point. Tours are also available further afield, to other resorts, monasteries and even Romania.

Kultura Tsentr (Cultural Centre)

The cultural centre provides culture of every conceivable kind, hosting events from traditional Bulgarian song and dance displays and classical music nights featuring the works of Strauss and Brahms, to magic and exotic animal shows. Look for the adverts on its doors or posted around town for details. Top pop bands also perform from time to time.

Luna Park

The park, in the centre of town, offers mini-golf, a small buggy track and donkey rides, as well as pleasant gardens through which to have a wander, and well-placed benches to park yourself on when you've had enough of wandering.

Spa treatments

Lie back, relax and allow yourself to be pampered. Whether you want to bust your cellulite, slow down the ageing process or just relax and de-stress, medical and beauty experts are on hand to cater to your every whim.

Watersports

Of course, most visitors to Albena expect to hit the waves at one time or another, whether that means having a gentle splash and a swim or indulging in some full-on extreme watersports. Water-skiing, parasailing, yachting, surfing, underwater fishing, jet-skiing, paragliding, sky-diving and scuba-diving through PADI are all on offer from the half a dozen or so sports centres on the beach. Tennis, football, riding and fitness clubs are also available for those who like their sports a little less terrifying.

AFTER DARK

Dining out in Albena can be a costly business. If you're staying in the resort it is unavoidable, but if you're just passing through it's worth eating before or after. Restaurants here tend to open and close frequently, so it's difficult to give accurate listings. Check the internet before you leave or ask other tourists for recommendations on arrival.

Restaurants

Poco Loco ££ With dancing waiters and waitresses, plus highly recommended food, Poco Loco is a family favourite, and not as expensive as some places in town. ⓐ Malibu Hotel ⓣ 0579 62279

Blue Sky £££ For a great view of the coast, head up to the 17th-floor terrace at the top of the Dobrudja Hotel. It's a smart place, the food is decent and the service excellent. The hotel also has a Chinese restaurant. ⓐ Dobrudja Hotel ⓣ 0579 62020

◔ *Parasailing and parasols at Albena*

Golden Sands

0 — 500 metres
0 — 500 yards

Albena

Berlin
Hotel

Amphitheatre ➌

Yacht
Port

Lilia Hotel ➎

Kaliakra Palace
Hotel

Varna ←

Black
Sea

Madara
Hotel

➍
➋
Admiral Hotel

Vladislav
Hotel ➓

Harry's Diving Centre

International
Hotel ➏
➐
➊
➑
➒

Aquapolis
Water Park

Hotel Perunika ⓫

Astera Hotel

N

Preslav Hotel

St Constantine
& Elena ↓

	Church
ℹ	Information
	Police Station
	Railway Stn
	Bus Stop
✉	Post Office
	Shopping

Golden Sands

If a British town had been shipped to Bulgaria and attached to the coast, Golden Sands would be it. Aside from the numerous British accents you will hear as you walk around, the shops and restaurants also advertise its Anglophile credentials. From tattoo and piercing parlours (with various comic variations on the spelling) to restaurants proudly proclaiming their full English breakfasts and Tetley tea, to a plethora of clothes shops and stalls selling everything from sunglasses, wallets and beach gear to England flags, football shirts and tracksuit tops with the name Victoria Beckham branded across them, this resort truly is a home from home for the Brits. British and English flags bedeck business after business, from the most cheap and cheerful pub to the most upmarket hotel. For the really homesick there are even a couple of McDonald's outlets.

Unlike its more sprawling counterpart in the southern resorts, Sunny Beach, Golden Sands is just about small enough to get around on foot. Much of its central strip is pedestrianised, and dotted with bars, restaurants, nightclubs, seaside entertainment and market stalls, with the hotels set slightly further back from the seafront but still affording excellent views. The streets in the resort do not have names and the buildings are not numbered, but it is not a difficult place to find your way around, with most of the attractions on or very close to the main strip. For unwilling walkers, a wheeled train will take you around the resort for a small sum. The emphasis is on fun and entertainment, and Golden Sands sometimes feels a bit like a fairground – an idea that is reinforced by its large beach Ferris wheel.

BEACHES

It's easy to see why so many tourists flock here. Golden Sands got its name for a reason – a beautiful, 5-km (3-mile) stretch of sand. The beach slopes gently and the sea has no cross-current, which makes it ideal for swimmers. Wide and clean with beautifully soft sand, it suits the active and inactive alike. The resort has pretty much every beach activity it's possible to think of, from volleyball and scuba-diving for the energetic to on-beach massage for those who just want to indulge themselves and be totally spoilt.

With an inexpensive 16-hole mini-golf green and small beachfront race track, there is plenty to occupy children, most of whom will be keen to try out the large Ferris wheel that dominates the Golden Sands skyline and serves as a useful orientation point. The small boating lake – a version of dodgems on water – is also popular with kids.

Parts of the beach are fenced off for private use and some areas charge a fee – look for the signs. Typically you will be charged if you sit among the umbrellas, while in front and behind them is free, public space. To sit on a mattress costs around 3 leva, renting a sunbed or umbrella roughly double that.

THINGS TO SEE & DO

Aquapolis Water Park

With slides and pools for both adults and children, a Jacuzzi and several eating options, this is a good alternative to the beach, particularly if the weather is bad. It's not cheap by Bulgarian standards – prices are based on height so be prepared to shell out if you have a tall family – but your entrance fee includes use of the inflatables and there's a discount after 16.00.

ⓐ On the road to Albena ⓣ 052 38 99 66 ⓦ www.aquapolis.net
ⓔ aquapolis@goldensands.bg.com ⓛ 10.00–18.30 ⓘ Admission charge

Casinos

As ubiquitous here as estate agents and fashion stores, casinos can be spotted fairly frequently at Golden Sands and elsewhere, with most hotels having their own casino on the premises. Make sure everyone in your group takes their passport if you go, as each person must register before being admitted.

Scuba-diving

Harry's Diving Centre meets all your sub-aquatic needs, whether you fancy seeing some archaeological sites on the seabed, a spot of underwater fishing or just want to learn the ropes. Boats go out to diving spots at Golden Sands, Cape Kaliakra and Cape Shabla. The centre offers PADI and SSI courses.

ⓐ Just off the central beach, close to the post office ⓣ 052 35 67 01
ⓦ www.goldensands.bg/padi ⓔ padi@goldensands.bg

⬥ *Splashing fun in the beachside pool*

TAKING A BREAK

Golden Sands has an array of bargain restaurants, all with the tourist in mind. Because the resort is large and self-contained, there is tight competition for your business, and prices vary little from one place to another – with one or two luxury exceptions. Most places that are suitable for taking a break in the day also do main meals at night, so they are listed together.

Dolphin £ ❶ Unpretentious national cuisine served in a large room with a nautical motif; a fishing boat hangs suspended above your heads. They have a non-smoking room. ⓐ Next to Astera Hotel ❶ 052 35 57 23 ❶ Cash only

Taj Mahal £ ❷ Ornately decorated Indian restaurant with an unmissable large gold Buddha. The food is well presented and recommended. ⓐ Next to Admiral Hotel ❶ 0886 60 00 30

Fisherman's Village ££ ❸ Huge fish restaurant with seafaring décor and views over the port. Authentic and fresh meals are served up to live music from the region, including Serbian, Croatian and Macedonian songs. ⓐ Yacht Port ❶ 052 35 68 95 ◐ 10.00–24.00

Gibraltar ££ ❹ Though it's not very well promoted or advertised, tourists repeatedly recommend this snack bar/restaurant for the standard of its food. You get great value for money and often some of the wine or beer accompanying your meal is thrown in for free. ⓐ Next to the Admiral Hotel

Tex Mex Rico ££ ❺ Live Latin music every evening from 19.30 with an in-house band and Mexican food, plus plenty of tequila to jolly things along. ⓐ In front of the Lilia Hotel ❶ 052 35 55 99 ◐ 09.00–24.00

Vectis Tavern ££ ❻ First and only English-owned and run restaurant in Golden Sands, serving Bulgarian food cooked to English standards. One of the main draws is the popular Bulgarian gypsy orchestra that plays there every night in season. ⓐ In between Astera and International Hotels ⓦ www.vectis-tavern.com ⓔ vectistavern@fsmail.net

Silver Gourmet £££ ❼ Gourmet food in a fabulously chic restaurant, done out in smart grey and white. Deer, veal, duck and buffalo dishes are among the many treats that will tempt bon viveurs. ⓐ Astera Hotel ⓣ 052 35 97 90 ⓛ 11.00–23.00

AFTER DARK

Bars & clubs

Arrogance Music Factory ❽ Stylish lounge and club, where you can listen to house, R&B, retro, pop or chill-out music as the mood takes you, in one of the four different rooms. ⓐ Astera Hotel Casino ⓦ www.arroganceclub.com ⓔ arrogance@ssi.bg ⓛ 22.00–06.00 ❗ Admission charge

Bonkers Disco ❾ Disco, house, Latino and oldies are on the playlist at this packed-out disco. ⓐ Next to Magoura Komplex ⓛ 22.00–05.00 ⓔ bonkers@disco.bg ❗ Admission charge

Club Masai ❿ With an African name and interior, this house and dance club is sometimes a stop for international DJs. ⓐ Behind Vladislav Hotel ⓔ masai@disco.bg ⓛ 22.00–late ❗ Admission charge

Muppet Karaoke Bar ⓫ Hugely popular seaside singalong joint with drinks offers most nights. ⓐ Hotel Perunika ⓣ 052 35 53 10 ⓦ www.muppetbar.com ⓔ contactcs@muppetbar.com

⬢ The name Golden Sands describes the resort perfectly

St Constantine & Elena

Verdant and compact, St Constantine & Elena feels more like a park than a commercial holiday resort. The oldest resort along Bulgaria's Black Sea coast, it was started almost 100 years ago. It was originally intended to host hospital patients, which may be the reason for the tranquil atmosphere it enjoys today, particularly in comparison to the bustling Golden Sands and Varna, its immediate neighbours to the north and south along the coast road.

It also differs from the other resorts in not having one main strip of shops along the beach, so lacks the buzz of some nearby places. This makes it suitable for older couples who are after a bit of peace and quiet, and who are willing to pay a bit more for the privilege. Varna is easily accessible by car or bus, so staying in St Constantine & Elena does not mean you will be cut off from the amenities of a large town.

BEACHES

St Constantine & Elena's small, relatively crowd-free beach can make a welcome change after the teeming Golden Sands. The surf at times gets a little rough, which deters swimmers, and watersports enthusiasts also go elsewhere, which preserves the calm of the beach for reading, sunbathing and relaxing. Its rocky areas and small pier make for picturesque photos. Unlike other beaches along the coast, it is divided into sections by a series of rocky patches, which affords a greater sense of privacy.

THINGS TO SEE & DO

Sports
Although far smaller and less developed than its surrounding resorts, there is still plenty in the way of physical activity in St Constantine & Elena. Scuba-diving, go-karting, fishing and scooter rental are all options,

● *Enjoy the food and the view at the Happy Bar & Grill*

the latter being a good way to get around the town, particularly as there are not too many cars about. Tennis courts are also available.

TAKING A BREAK

Perhaps because of its small size, St Constantine & Elena is not well served for restaurants and the places you do find tend to be on the pricey side. For this reason, tourists often head back to nearby Varna for dinner. However, there are a couple of places that serve a decent-value meal.

Happy Bar & Grill £ Outlet of the popular American-style diner chain. Bright and breezy service, musical instruments and Hollywood memorabilia on the walls and quality far higher than the bargain prices suggest. From salads and snacks to main course, everything is great. ⓐ Opposite Grand Hotel Varna ① 052 36 13 88 ⓒ 09.00–23.00

Snack Bar Delphin ££ Serves full meals as well as ice cream. ⓐ Beachside ⓒ 11.30–22.30

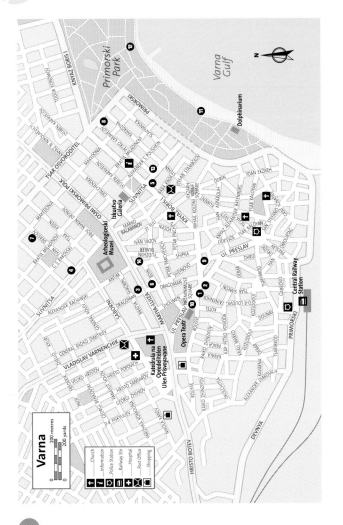

Varna

Varna has truly embraced the foreign influxes of tourists and property hunters who have made their way to Bulgaria's Black Sea coast. Your first likely port of call when visiting any of the resorts in the northern cluster, the town has become something of a hub. Both a resort and a flourishing city in its own right, it has the charm of a holiday destination and all the modern comforts of a busy town, such as great shops and fantastic food.

In some ways, Varna almost feels like home. The names that you're used to seeing on your local high street – Benetton, Mango – are here, along with several high-class designer stores. It's certainly difficult to see any traces of the Communist regime that fell two decades ago in the swish shops of this city. Another unavoidable symbol is the Union Flag (or Union Jack), usually heralding an estate agent catering to the many Brits who want to make the Black Sea coast their second home.

Despite its size, many of Varna's highlights can be seen on foot. Indeed, in the heart of the city there is no other way: the central area, leading up to the impressive cathedral, is pedestrianised, giving it a peaceful, relaxed ambience that belies the town's status as a thriving port and business centre. Fountains and small, well-tended gardens add to the effect. This traffic-free zone is brimming with cafés and restaurants, almost all of which have outside terraces that make great spots for people-watching.

THINGS TO SEE & DO

Arheologiceski Muzei (Archaeological Museum)

Housed in an atmospheric former school set in some gardens, like the Art Gallery, this place features religious icons as well as artefacts throughout several rooms.

ⓐ Mariya Luiza 41, on corner with Bul Slivnitsa ❶ 052 23 70 57
ⓦ www.varna-bg.com/museums/archaeology/enexhibit/index.htm
🕒 10.00–17.00 Tues–Sun, closed Mon (summer); 10.00–17.00 Tues–Sat, closed Sun & Mon (winter) ❶ Admission charge

◆ *Once a school, now the archaeological museum*

Dolphinarium

Aquatic fun for the kids. Half-hour displays of juggling, dancing and acrobatics from the most popular sea creature.

ⓐ Sea Gardens ❶ 052 30 21 99 ● Shows at 11.00, 14.00 & 15.30 Tues–Sun, closed Mon, June–Aug; 11.00 & 15.00 Tues–Sun, closed Mon, Sept–May
❶ Admission charge

Izkustvo Galeria (Art Gallery)

Round the back of the Methodist Church, the gallery displays mainly modern art, from traditional interwar paintings, sculptures and portraits to more contemporary pop-art-style exhibits. Upstairs houses the permanent exhibition, with works by both international and Bulgarian artists. Downstairs is the guest exhibition, with pieces that can be yours to take away for anything from 100 to 1,000 leva.

ⓐ Lyuben Karavelov 1 ❶ 052 61 23 63 ● 10.00–18.00 Tues–Sun, closed Mon ❶ Admission charge

Katedrala na Opredelitelen Ulen Prisvoyavane (Cathedral of the Assumption)

Probably Varna's best known piece of architecture, the 19th-century cathedral is equally impressive inside with its ornate gold carvings, icons and throne. Outside is a small collection of stalls where old women knit and sell simultaneously. Babies' bootees and socks seem to be the main merchandise on offer, but the larger marketplace across the street has a far wider range, from fruit, vegetables and spices to wallets, soft toys and Russian dolls of George Bush and Vladimir Putin.

ⓐ Pl Mitropolit Simeon

TAKING A BREAK

Restaurants & cafés
Happy Bar & Grill £ ❶ Superb cheap and cheerful American-style diner chain that is brightly decorated with musical instruments and film memorabilia. Great food and upbeat atmosphere – a real bargain.

ⓐ Ul Preslav 11 ☏ 052 60 25 41 ⓦ www.happy.bg ⓔ office@happy.bg
🕐 07.00–24.00

Montrey ££ ❷ Large café-restaurant overlooking Varna's central precinct, ideal for relaxing and watching the world go by. Follow a sandwich, salad, pizza or pasta with one of their desserts, temptingly on display. ⓐ Ul Preslav 42 ☏ 052 60 24 18 🕐 09.00–23.00 ❶ Cash only

🔺 *Watch dolphins display their talents at the Dolphinarium*

AFTER DARK

Restaurants

Dragoman Bistro ££ ❸ Lamb and rabbit dishes feature among the Bulgarian, Italian and international options on offer, with a wide range of wines to choose from to help wash them down. A fireplace adds ambience inside, and there are some tables outside. ⓐ Ul Dragoman 43 ⓣ 052 62 16 88 ⓛ 08.30–23.00

Kashtata sas Slanceto ££ ❹ Fish specialities and veal are among the top attractions at this international themed place, not to mention its large, leafy terrace. ⓐ Ul Tsar Asen 3 ⓣ 052 60 01 81 ⓛ 10.00–24.00 ⓘ Cash only

Panorama restaurant ££ ❺ While the food is fairly standard meat-based Bulgarian cuisine, this restaurant, on the top floor of the Cherno More Hotel, is worth it for the spectacular view of the city alone. ⓐ Bul Slivnitsa 33 ⓣ 052 23 21 15 ⓛ 11.30–24.00 ⓘ Cash only

Pri Chuchura ££ ❻ For a taste of traditional Bulgaria that has nothing to do with tourist trails or property booms, this is the place. From the folk costumes and tapestry on the walls to the food on your plate, this is home cooking through and through. ⓐ Ul Dragoman 11 ⓣ 0897 87 06 12 ⓛ 10.00–24.00

Za Priateli ££ ❼ The name means For Friends, and with its budget prices and unfussy atmosphere this pizzeria is a good place to come in a group. ⓐ Ul Makedonia 82 ⓣ 052 60 28 98 ⓔ zapriateli@gmail.com

Capitol £££ ❽ This classy restaurant limits itself to a few, very well-done dishes. The European cuisine is complemented by a wide range of Bulgarian and international wine, all served in a sophisticated dining atmosphere. ⓐ Ul Petko Karavelov 40 ⓣ 052 68 80 00 ⓦ www.capitol.bg ⓔ office@capitol.bg ⓛ 11.00–23.00

Musala Palace £££ ❾ Quite possibly Varna's best restaurant. Exemplary service, delightful gourmet food and classic baroque interior make dining here a rare pleasure. VIPs eat here and it is easy to see why. Highly recommended. ⓐ Pl Musala 3 ❶ 052 66 41 96 Ⓦ www.musalapalace.bg ❶ 06.00–23.00

Theatre

Opera Teatr (Opera Theatre) ❿ Varna's unmistakable pink theatre hosts several shows a week, including opera, classical, rock and popular music plus ballet, all at bargain prices. ⓐ Pl Nezavisimost ❶ 052 22 30 39 Ⓦ www.operavarna.bg ⓔ office@operavarna.bg

Bars & clubs

Boogie Bar ⓫ Bright and cheerful beachfront bar pumping out retro and Latino music as the tequila flows thick and fast. ⓐ Coastal Avenue ❶ 052 64 50 50 ❶ 22.00–04.00

4as Pik ⓬ Dimly lit night spot where the resident DJ plays a mixture of pop, retro and Balkans music. ⓐ Coastal Avenue ❶ 0899 84 29 96 Ⓦ www.4aspik.com ⓔ 4aspik@ssi.bg ❶ 22.00–06.00 ❶ Admission charge

O'Neills ⓭ Varna has not escaped the global proliferation of Irish pubs. Listen to live performances from Bulgarian, American and Irish musicians as you sup your pint of the black stuff or your whiskey. ⓐ Bul Slivnitza 7 ❶ 052 61 45 86 ⓔ oneillsbg@yahoo.com ❶ 18.00–02.00

Royal Classic ⓮ Intimate piano and live music bar, with veteran acts and up-and-coming musicians all taking their turn at tinkling the ivories. ⓐ Ul Shipka 18 ❶ 052 60 15 96 ❶ 22.00–03.00 ❶ Admission charge

Sunny Beach

For pure pleasure-seekers, Sunny Beach is a purpose-built paradise. The largest Bulgarian Black Sea coast resort, it is made up almost entirely of hotels, restaurants and entertainment facilities, all geared to the convenience of the holidaymaker. Whether you've come on holiday for the thrills of watersports, to party until dawn in thumping nightspots or just to lie on one of the most beautiful stretches of sand on the coast, Sunny Beach obliges you. This is what makes it such a good choice for family groups: while there is plenty to keep children entertained, like special pools, slides, bouncy castles and mini-golf, adults are also well catered for.

As it is the biggest resort on the Black Sea coast, if you want to explore the whole town you really need a car. But the bus service runs fairly late, and in truth there's little need to see everything. Sunny Beach has so many hotels, restaurants, discos and beach activities that, wherever you are based, you are likely to be within easy reach of everything the sunseeker needs. The main action is centred on a mile-long pedestrianised strip full of eating and drinking options, as well as various market stalls. If you do want to go further afield you can hire a bicycle to get around, or even let someone else do the work by taking a rickshaw ride or the mini-train.

In the unlikely event that you do run out of things to occupy yourself, or if you just fancy seeing a bit more of the country, you're well placed to do so. Because Sunny Beach is so geared up to tourists, many visitors choose to use it as a base from which to travel around various parts of Bulgaria. Trips by bus and boat are available not only to the resorts in the vicinity, but also further afield to Sofia, Plovdiv and Varna among other places, which means that in between lapping up the sun you can take in your fair share of culture – museums, cities and monasteries.

BEACHES

Sunny Beach did not get its name for nothing. The sun seems to shine even when the rest of the country gets rain. The wide beach stretches off

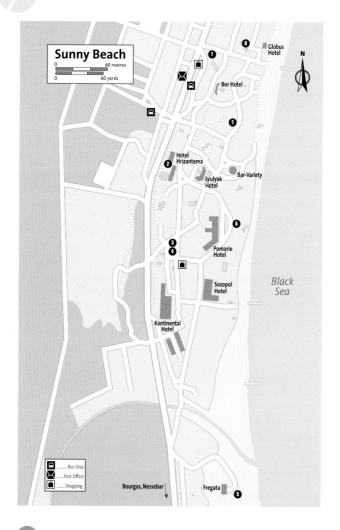

Sunny Beach

0 ———— 60 metres
0 ———— 60 yards

Globus Hotel
Bor Hotel
Hotel Hrizantema
Lyulyak Hotel
Bar-Variety
Pomorie Hotel
Sozopol Hotel
Kontinental Hotel
Black Sea
Bourgas, Nessebar
Fregata

Bus Stop
Post Office
Shopping

towards the cliffs in the distance – mile after mile of soft, grainy sand, perfect for long walks. Clean and safe, the beach is a worthy winner of the Blue Flag award. There is no shortage of other pursuits, such as fishing, volleyball and a wealth of watersports. Water-skiing, parasailing, hang-gliding, plus boat trips from banana boats and pedaloes to yachts – it's difficult to think of a beach activity that isn't on offer. While some small businesses have set up on the beach, there are too few for it to feel cluttered or overly commercial.

Because the beach faces east, early birds can watch the sun rise over the warm sea, with the cliffs off to the left. With its rare sand dunes and as the habitat of several protected species of plant, Sunny Beach also has plenty to interest nature lovers.

Thanks to the mountains, which form a picturesque backdrop to the far left end of beach as you look out to sea, the resort gets a fresh breeze that keeps sunbathers from scorching. The sea is warm, gentle and safe with no unpredictable tides or nasty surprises like jellyfish. A flag system is in operation to indicate how safe it is to swim: green means fine for everyone, yellow indicates that only competent swimmers should go in the water and red prohibits swimming altogether.

Of course, with so much to recommend it, Sunny Beach does see large numbers of tourists. While that makes for a great atmosphere in the bars and discos long after the sun has gone down, it can be less welcome when you're trying to find a spot on the sand. For a little more privacy and space, walk a little way north along the beach. The majority of hotels are concentrated in the south, which is why the southern part of the beach can fill up quicker.

THINGS TO SEE & DO

Watersports

As a beacon in the area for adrenalin junkies, it would almost be quicker to list the watersports that you can't do at Sunny Beach. Surfing, water-skiing, parasailing, hang-gliding and scuba-diving are all on offer, and you can hit the waves in anything from a banana or rowing boat to a chartered yacht. The bonus is that, thanks to the cheap petrol powering the boats, plus the country's low prices in general, the most extravagant water-based pursuit is a bargain compared to what you'd be paying at the equivalent Western European resort.

⬤ *Stay on your toes with beach volleyball*

TAKING A BREAK

Café Amadeus £££ ❶   Coffee and tea connoisseurs will be in heaven in this classy café, which serves exotic brews from all over: the coffees hail from Cuba, Peru and Zimbabwe among others, and Chinese Ceylon is one of the tempting teas. It's not cheap, but if you want a little sophistication after the beach and clubbing treadmill you will find it here. ⓐ Hotel Iberostar ⏰ 10.30–22.30

AFTER DARK

Restaurants & cafés

Sunny Beach is entirely dedicated to summer season tourists. The season runs from around May to early October, and from this time onwards many places begin to close for the winter.

Bar Sante ££ ❷   Cheerfully decorated diner serving a good selection of Italian favourites, plus chicken dishes, curries, omelettes and salads. There are plenty of wines to go with your meal.
ⓐ Hotel Hrizantema ☎ 0885 66 56 56 ⏰ 09.00–23.00, May–end Oct
❶ Cash only

The Corner Pub ££ ❸   Part of the Meridian Hotel, this huge pub is also a restaurant, serving English and international cuisine from fish specials, grilled meat and roast dinners to spaghetti bolognese. With its pool table, football shirts and flags, plus large screen and Sky TV, it's a favourite among Brits. ⓐ Meridian Hotel ⏰ 08.30–last customer
❶ Cash only

Meridian £££ ❹   Smart poolside restaurant serving Mexican food, curries, pizza, T-bone steak plus various milkshakes and shots. The hotel that it is part of also has a rooftop restaurant with panoramic views.
ⓐ Meridian Hotel ⏰ 10.30–22.00, May–Oct

Clubs & bars

Elephant ££ ❺   Set as it is in a tent, and with its name, you could almost be in India rather than Eastern Europe. Unusual beachfront club that delivers something a bit different. ⓐ Cacao Beach
ⓦ www.elephant.kvartira.bg/den.html

Lazur ££ ❻   Despite only opening recently, this disco has already attracted a loyal fan base. Three floors, a pool and garden and 11 bars should keep you entertained for a while. ⓐ Opposite Pomorie Hotel
ⓣ 0889 93 23 85 ⓛ 22.30–late ❶ Admission charge

XL Disco ££ ❼   Packed and popular disco pumping out commercial and R&B music, plus techno, trance, soul and retro. Its non-smoking room is another draw for foreign tourists. ⓐ Kuban Hotel ⓣ 0888 31 53 14
ⓛ 22.00–late ❶ Admission charge

Makalali £££ ❽   African themed nightclub with big zebra print sofas, drapes and pine decorations. By day it operates as a relaxing chill-out zone, at night a DJ spins house, retro and commercial tunes.
ⓐ Behind Globus Hotel ⓣ 0898 58 13 85 ⓔ makalali_club@mail.bg

⬤ Take a break from the beach

Nessebar

It's easy to see why Nessebar (sometimes written as Nessebur, or other variations) is a UNESCO-protected site. It has retained not only many remnants of its history, but also its atmosphere of a picturesque fishing village. Famous as much for its 19th-century wooden architecture as for its cluster of small medieval churches, it feels a world away from the more commercial resorts, and its relative isolation has served it well. The old town is almost like an island, set on a peninsula connected to the nearby Sunny Beach by one main road, which means that you rarely have to walk more than a minute or so before you're confronted with dazzling blue sea. It's a small settlement, entirely navigable on foot, and indeed many areas are almost entirely car free, which only adds to its island charm.

Although Nessebar is by no means lacking in the facilities that the visitor needs, such as hotels, restaurants, museums and souvenir shops, it has a markedly different feel from its larger neighbour. While Sunny Beach is modern, large and purpose-built, Nessebar has grown naturally and organically, its small size protecting it from the excesses of developers.

The two main draws are fish and history. Little boats line the shore and the plethora of tempting fish restaurants that look out to the sea serve up today's catch. There are many places where you can take a seat and watch the town's fishermen going about their work. Anywhere you wander, you'll be surrounded by a sense of the island's past. Whether it's the remnants of historical ruins and old churches, the timeless craft of the fishermen or the absence of huge hotels, in Nessebar the 21st century feels miles away.

BEACHES

Some visitors rate Nessebar's beaches as the best in Bulgaria – with it being a peninsula the beachgoer is spoilt for choice. Owing to the town's popularity, its vast stretch of fine golden sand can get crowded,

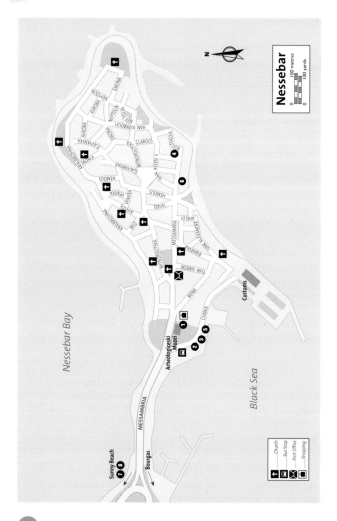

particularly later in the morning when the day-trippers begin to pile in. Some visitors recommend the beach area in the new town.

For watersports, most people head to the nearby Sunny Beach. Nessebar is so steeped in the atmosphere of an old fishing village that one of the main pleasures of its seashore is watching the fishermen at work, and the small boats bobbing by the harbour.

THINGS TO SEE & DO

Arheologiceski Muzei (Archaeological Museum)
Appropriately set among some of the town's ruins, the museum houses stone carvings, masks, statues, urns, coins, jewellery and anchors, many of which are over 2,000 years old. Downstairs is a collection of icons.
ⓐ Inside the old town gateway ⓛ 09.00–18.00 Mon–Fri, 09.00–17.00 Sat & Sun

Churches
Anyone who enjoys church architecture will be in their element in Nessebar. Built over the centuries, the various examples reflect the influences of whichever group was in ascendancy at the time. Ceramics and frescoes are some of the highlights.

TAKING A BREAK

Klio ice cream parlour ££ ❶ If you like your sundaes accompanied by loud dance music, try sitting inside Klio. If you prefer peace and quiet, choose one of the outside tables overlooking the sea. ⓐ By the Archaeological Museum ⓛ 08.00–24.00

AFTER DARK

Restaurants
There is a cluster of restaurants at the point where you enter the town, by the bus stop. All have a sea view and tables outside. Have a walk

⬥ *Nessebar has some fine examples of Byzantine architecture*

around and you're bound to find something that suits you, and the competition means that prices are fairly standard. As you go further into Nessebar, the next main eating area is around the Ethnographical Museum. It's a small resort, so most places only take cash for the moment, although this is likely to change over the coming years.

Corona ££ ❷ Chic eatery with a sea view and impressive selection of fish and chicken mains. The oven and BBQ outside add to the atmosphere. ⓐ By the town bus stop ❶ 0888 20 65 73 ⏱ 09.00–24.00

Flaman ££ ❸ Fish restaurant serving up almost anything that swims – salmon, shark, blue fish, scad and crayfish are all on the menu, and there is a tank of live crabs from which to select your dinner if you want ultimate freshness. Other cosmopolitan treats such as blue cheese salad also mark this place out from the competition. ⓐ By the bus stop ⏱ 09.00–21.00

Kapitanska Sreshta ££ ❹ A charming fish restaurant in what is possibly the best location on the island, as well as being the oldest house. A big keg, fishing boat and three model drunken sailors liven the place up. The extensive menu features salmon, octopus, mussels and crab. ⓐ By the Ethnographical Museum (currently closed) ❶ 0554 42124 ⓦ http://kapitanska-sreshta.sea-hotels-bg.com ⏱ 10.00–around 23.00 ❶ Cash only

Kos Greek Tavern ££ ❺ Unmistakably done out in blue and white and decorative fishing nets, Kos serves up Greek-style specialities such as stuffed aubergines, grilled octopus and Greek salad, plus standard Black Sea favourites pizza, pasta and English breakfasts. ⓐ By the bus stop ⏱ 09.00–23.00

Sevina ££ ❻ Glass-fronted restaurant overlooking the sea, where you can munch on salads, seafood or national dishes while sipping a cocktail or two. Its nearby sister restaurant is Zornitza. ⓐ Ul Messambria, next to

Community Centre ① 0554 42603 ② zornitza_nessebar@abv.bg
① 08.00–01.00

Victoria ££ ❼   A mixture of international and local dishes served either
inside or on a long terrace. ② Ul Zornitza 5 ① 0554 42693
① 09.00–24.00 ① Cash only

Clubs & bars
Xtreme ££ ❽   Lounge-style club playing house, retro and commercial
tracks. ② Ul Han Krum 11 ① 0897 84 48 66/7 ① 08.00–late

● *Seafood restaurants are excellent and plentiful*

Pomorie

Pomorie is nestled between the sea on one side and Lake Pomorie – a salt lagoon that is famous in the area for its 2,000-year-old mud treatments – on the other. Its other chief attraction is its bird-watching opportunities.

Despite its small size, the town has a sophisticated social scene and nightlife. As such, it would suit couples who want to escape the tourist hordes, without giving up a decent choice of restaurants and bars. High-quality grapes grow in the region, so trying the local wine is certainly something to put on your to-do list. The main places to eat, drink and dance are in or around the pedestrianised area ul Knyaz Boris, which is marked by the **Church of the Nativity**.

For more information about what's on offer in the town, the small tourist office can give suggestions and a useful map. ⓐ Ul Kraybrezhna, close to the beach ⓛ 08.00–22.00, May–Sept

BEACH

Not being a major resort, Pomorie's beach can provide some welcome space and privacy in high season. The water is shallow, and therefore suitable for all swimmers. Wooden barriers have been constructed to prevent sea erosion. There's a pier where aspiring fishermen try their luck.

THINGS TO DO

Bird-watching

Pomorie Lake, by the Salt Museum, is a top spot for twitchers and has also made great strides in breeding and protection. From six pairs of nesting terns in 1996, the number reached 450 in 2002. Over 240 species of birds frequent the area, five of which are threatened throughout the world.

Sol Muzei (Salt Museum)

Dedicated to the area's main product, this quirky little museum explains how salt production technology has developed from ancient times, and features videos in English, old photos and live demonstrations.
ⓐ Behind the stadium ⓣ 0596 25344 ⓔ alas@unacs.bg

St Rojdestvo Bogorodichno (Church of the Nativity)

This is the town's central church, which is much more cavernous inside than it appears from the exterior. With its candles and chanting, it is dark and particularly atmospheric.
ⓐ Ul Knyaz Boris ⓛ 07.00–13.00 & 15.30–18.00

AFTER DARK

Restaurants & cafés

Paradise Café ££ Trendy orange café, serving coffees, milkshakes, cocktails and desserts to Pomorie's smart set. ⓐ Opposite the Church of the Nativity ⓛ 07.00–24.00

St George ££ Traditional and upmarket hotel restaurant, done out in an English style with photos on the walls. Serves veal, fish, pizza and pasta in a classy, serene atmosphere. ⓐ Ul Javarov 15 ⓣ 0596 24411 ⓦ www.st-george-bg.com ⓛ 08.00–24.00 ⓘ Open all year round

Sozopol

Popular with artists and writers for over a hundred years, Sozopol is the top cultural spot of the southern group of Black Sea resorts. Its museums, galleries, art and music clubs, not forgetting a smattering of small, pretty churches, create an air of sophistication lacking in some of the more tourist-oriented resorts. Shoppers in Sozopol are more likely to be offered a portrait by one of the street artists than a replica football shirt. Concerts take place throughout the summer at the town's amphitheatre, and the same venue hosts the main event in Sozopol's cultural calendar, the Appolonia Festival.

A fishing village, the town is pretty with narrow, sloping, cobbled streets that wind between two-storey overhanging houses. Besides the hotels and restaurants that cater to the modern traveller, it's easy to imagine that very little else has changed over the years. A pleasant park, commemorating the area's fallen soldiers, adds to the sense of history.

BEACHES

Sozopol is made up of two main sections. On the mainland is the Harmanite area, an up-to-date district where you will find most of the hotels, as well as South or Harmanite Beach. It's the biggest stretch of sand in the town itself, so can be a better bet in the peak months of July and August. Lifeguards patrol the seafront; the sea has currents and can get rough at times. Keep an eye out for the red flag, which indicates that swimming is dangerous. Umbrellas and chairs are available for a small fee, and there's a separate area for everyone else. Topless, but not nude, sunbathing is permitted.

The Old Town is on the peninsula, which curves round to an easterly point, and here you'll find the popular Central Beach, which can get busy in high season. The same system applies as at Harmanite Beach, with a charge for the use of umbrellas and chairs, which have their own area. Again, topless sunbathing only is permitted.

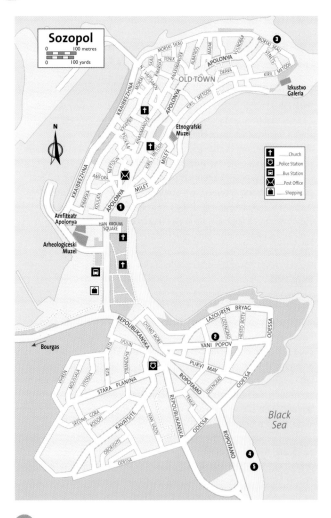

Sozopol

| 0 | 100 metres |
| 0 | 100 yards |

OLD TOWN

Izkustvo
Galeria

Etnografski
Muzei

Amfiteatr
Apolonya

Arheologiceski
Muzei

HAN KROUM
SQUARE

← Bourgas

Black
Sea

	.........Church
	.........Police Station
	.........Bus Station
	.........Post Office
	.........Shopping

A third option exists for those who like a little more privacy. Three km (2 miles) north of town is the Gold Fish campsite, which has a private beach, accessible for a small sum. There is also a charge for use of an umbrella. Although not officially permitted, nude sunbathing is generally more acceptable here than at the two beaches in town.

THINGS TO SEE & DO

Amfiteatr Apolonya (Apollonia Amphitheatre)

While Sozopol's amphitheatre might have the atmosphere of somewhere more ancient, it was in fact built relatively recently for the Apollonia festival (see page 107). It also gets some use throughout the rest of the summer as a concert venue. The festival website hosts a comprehensive programme of events including ticket details.

ⓐ By the Archaeological Museum and the library ⓣ 02 980 7833
ⓦ www.apollonia.bg

Arheologiceski Muzei (Archaeological Museum)

Pottery, pictures and icons dating back over 2,000 years. Old anchors are among the more memorable exhibits.

ⓐ Khan Krum 2 ⓣ 0550 2226 ⓛ 08.00–18.00 (summer); 08.00–12.00 & 13.15–17.00 Mon–Fri, closed Sat & Sun (winter) ⓘ Admission charge

Etnografski Muzei (Ethnographical Museum)

Set among the remains of a well and a fortress wall and tower, the museum really feels steeped in history. Inside are old artefacts showcasing the town's past as a Greek colony and the fishing that has sustained it.

ⓐ Ul Milet 50 ⓣ 0550 22267 ⓔ office@sozopol-foundation.com
ⓛ 08.00–17.00

Izkustvo Galeria (Art Gallery)

The fishing theme continues with historical and more contemporary art, housed in the town's former high school.

ⓐ Kiril i Metodii 70 ⓣ 0550 2202 ⓛ 08.30–18.30

◆ *Traditional housing at Sozopol*

AFTER DARK

Restaurants & cafés

Katerini £ ❶ Friendly, informal service and a huge range of Bulgarian dishes, with a few international favourites thrown in for good measure. ⓐ Ul Apolonya 5 ❶ 0550 23650

Kavaler ££ ❷ Intimate eatery serving seafood, including indulgent treats like caviar. ⓐ Ul Yani Popov 21 ❶ 0550 23646 ⓔ kavalerbg@abv.bg

Windmill ££ ❸ Popular Bulgarian restaurant with meat dishes that are set alight before your eyes, folk shows and dancing. ⓐ Ul Morski Skali 27 ❶ 0550 22844 ⓔ wm.soz.bg@abv.bg ⏰ 10.00–24.00

Bars & clubs

Club Cult ££ ❹ Playing everything from retro classics to house, dance, soul and R&B, this place is worth a visit for the barmen doing their best impersonation of Tom Cruise in *Cocktail*. ⓐ Harmanite Beach ❶ 0887 77 71 27 ❶ Admission charge

Havana ££ ❺ Pizzeria and bar in one, famed for its wild dancing plus its patio and swimming pool. ⓐ Harmanite Beach ❶ 0550 22209 ⏰ 24 hours (summer)

Primorsko

With its combination of bustling nightspots and a wide range of water-based activities, Primorsko is ideal for young adults who want to wring every bit of fun out of their holiday, both day and night. It's not the most upmarket of resorts, but that attracts a young, fun-loving crowd, and Primorsko regulars rave about the wild discos and cheap tequila.

BEACHES

With a grassy knoll running down to it and plenty of trees dotted around, Primorsko's beach has a natural, roughhewn quality to it. At the northern end, the choppy sea attracts windsurfers, while the calmer waters in the southern part are better for swimmers. Primorsko's bargain prices do mean that the beaches can fill up quickly. Nearby options for those wanting a little more space are Perla beach, accessible by the small wheeled train, and the International Youth Centre, a hotel complex just over a mile south of the town. Watch out for a red flag, which means the water is too rough for swimming.

THINGS TO SEE & DO

Diving
Poseidon diving centre offers a range of aquatic activities in the nearby area.
ⓐ Kiril i Metodij 16 ❶ 0888 93 51 24 ⓔ info@poseidonet.cz
🕙 18.00–22.00

AFTER DARK

Restaurants & cafés
The Old Windmill £££ Large, simple eatery offering Bulgarian cuisine, sometimes accompanied by live music. ⓐ Ul Treti Mart 50
❶ 0899 84 87 47

Clubs & bars

Impulse ££ A Primorsko favourite, Impulse opened a couple of years ago and has been pulling in an up-for-it crowd ever since. ⓐ Ul Kostadinov ⓣ 0550 32507

Luxor ££ Gloriously tacky and hugely popular disco playing house, dance and commercial tracks. Things can get rather raucous – it's not a place for wallflower types. ⓐ On the beach, look for the sphinx ⓣ 0888 51 51 20 ⓘ Admission charge

● *The church of Saint Stefan at Primorsko*

Ahtopol

If the seaside to you is nothing to do with jet skis, all-day English breakfasts and lilos, and more about tranquillity and traditional coastal activities like fishing, Ahtopol might suit you. A long way south of the main stretch of resorts clustered around Sunny Beach, it's only around 18 km (11 miles) from the Turkish border. But don't go expecting to see a huge outside influence; the town is isolated enough to have its own character that differs from its large neighbour or the usual effects of tourism.

In Ahtopol, it is still possible to take a stroll and pass a donkey casually ambling the other way along the street. From the football pitch at the edge of town all the way to the beach, this is a place that has not been wholly subsumed by the tourist bug. Of course there are hotels, restaurants and bars where a visitor can enjoy a drink or a meal while looking out to sea, but you won't see the usual shops of the more businesslike holiday resorts here.

Instead, you will find a small, self-contained town, which just happens to be by the sea and have some fantastic views of the rugged coastline. Anyone who does tire of the solitude and wants a taste of city life can book a trip out on one of the buses that serve Sofia and Bourgas several times a day.

BEACHES

Far from being packed with foreign tourists, your fellow beachgoers are more likely to be veteran fishermen just sitting and shooting the breeze. Set back from the beach is a pleasant and quiet park, popular with the old people of the town. But Ahtopol is not entirely conservative – the northern section of the beach is popular with nude bathers. If you do decide to bare all, make sure not to forget your wallet – there is a charge of a few leva for a sunshade.

◗ *Fishing boats at Ahtopol*

AFTER DARK

Restaurants & bars

Magic Café £ Well-stocked and tended traditional Bulgarian bar overlooking the sea. ⓐ At the pier 🕓 08.00–24.00

Kasablanka Restaurant ££ Bulgarian and Greek cuisine, including fish, roast lamb, pork or chicken and mussels. You can even take your meal on the beach itself. ⓐ Lola Garden Hotel, ul Preobrazenska 7, Harmanite Beach ⓣ 0554 62020 ⓦ www.lolagarden.com ⓔ office@lolagarden.com 🕓 10.00–24.00

⊙ *Flying high over the Black Sea*

⬤ *The lake and marshland of Srebarna National Park*

Excursions in the north

Srebarna National Park

Up near the Romanian border, a visit to Srebarna, though it might be off the beaten track, rewards both keen twitchers and any lovers of wide open spaces. A large area of freshwater lake and marshland, adjacent to the River Danube, it is accessible by bus from the nearest town but is better seen by car if you want to get around the 600-hectare (1,483-acre) site. There are wildlife trails to follow, and it is also possible to take guided or solo tours. Once part of Romanian territory, the area has been a national park for nearly 60 years and is on the UNESCO World Heritage list.

Top attraction has to be the birds. Around 90 different species have made the lake their home, and another 80 pass through on what is called the Via Pontica, a migration route for birds between Europe and Africa. The Dalmatian pelican, great egret, night heron, purple heron, glossy ibis and white spoonbill are just a few of the treats awaiting ornithologists. There is something to be seen for most of the year, whether it is pelicans in the spring, egrets in summer or geese in winter. If you are brave, try climbing up one of the somewhat rickety viewing posts – and bring your binoculars.

But birds are not the only things that seek the protection of this remote area. There are believed to be 39 species of mammal, 21 types of reptile and amphibians and 10 fish species also in the area, some of which are facing extinction outside it. The stuffed creatures in the small museum will not be to everyone's taste, but the facility does give further information on some of the species you might spot if you're lucky, and its staff can suggest the best way to see the area, which can be quite a challenge due to its size.

But even if you can't tell your bluethroat from your greylag goose, the park has a strong appeal. Walking the narrow tracks with a canopy of trees above your head, at times you can hear nothing but distant birdsong.

 Srebarna National Park is to the north of the road between Silistra and Ruse, which runs alongside the Danube – look for signs to either Srebarna or Vetren, the nearby villages. From Silistra, which is 17 km (10½ miles) away, you can pick up bus 222 from the bus station, and the area is also served by buses travelling between Silistra and Ruse

THINGS TO SEE & DO

Prirodonauchen Muzei (Natural History Museum)
While the stuffed exhibits are not to everyone's taste, the museum covers the area's wildlife fairly well and gives you a clue as to what you can expect to see on your visit.
ⓐ Srebarna village, follow the signs ⓒ 09.00–12.00 & 14.00–18.00

AFTER DARK

Kalimaritsa ££ Traditional, hearty meals are just the ticket after a day spent rambling or bird-watching in the reserve. ⓐ Ul Stratsin 17, Vetren
ⓣ 085 14515

Kaliakra Nature Reserve

If you like your nature untamed and elemental, it's worth making the journey north to the Kaliakra Nature Reserve. Cape Kaliakra juts out into the sea some 49 km (30 miles) up the coast from Balchik, and is like another place and time from the bustling resorts that dot the country's Black Sea coastline. Getting there is not easy – you either need to drive yourself, go with an organised tour group from Balchik or other resorts in the area, or be prepared for a lot of walking. But those who go to the bother are rewarded with one of Bulgaria's most captivating wildernesses.

Get lucky, and from the clifftops you may spot a bottlenose dolphin plying the sea below, or even a rare shag. The cape is also a must on the

⬥ *The glossy ibis is just one of the birds that visit this area*

BIRD-WATCHING

Srebarna, the Bourgas Lakes, Cape Kaliakra and Pomorie are among the many excellent areas in Bulgaria for bird-watching. If you're new to twitching, here are a few tips to get you started.

Do your homework beforehand. Gen up on what kind of birds you're likely to see – and that means reading the descriptions as well as looking at the pictures. Make sure you're well acquainted with any common species. Birds tend to be more active early in the day, particularly in warm weather, so it's worth setting the alarm and making an early start. Just before sunset is also a good time to spot some types.

The main thing is to have a decent pair of binoculars. It's worth buying the best you can, but there's no need to break the bank – a secondhand pair will do the job just as well. Listening is just as important as looking. Birdsong may be your first clue that a particular bird is in your area, and some birds are far more likely to reveal themselves by sound than by sight.

It goes without saying that the birds you might spot out in the wild will be less comfortable with your presence than the pigeons in your local park. Wear clothes that blend in with the natural environment, and that won't make a noise when you move. Conceal yourself by standing by a tree or in foliage. Keep your voice down and move around slowly.

Have patience. Even expert twitchers can struggle to recognise and place the birds they spot. Enjoy the experience and don't expect to master the skill straightaway. Finally, it goes without saying that you should interfere with the birds as little as possible – this goes double when they are around their nests or with their young.

birdwatcher's list of places to go around the Black Sea coast, due to the ideal breeding conditions it affords. Whatever time of year you go, you should be able to spot birds of one kind or another. But even if you don't see any of the wildlife whose habitats are carefully preserved at the site, the reserve rewards your visit with the centuries-old ruins of churches, wells and castle walls, as well as its bracing, *Wuthering Heights*-style atmosphere. The cape's rural, desolate position was the very reason that it was chosen for the construction of Tirisis, an ancient fortress that was used by the various races ruling the area over the centuries.

Amble along the rustic, irregular pathways that run along the top of limestone rocks, around 60 to 70 m (200 to 230 ft) high, and you could just as easily be in the 1st century as the 21st century. Cars, trains, all modernity is forgotten as you get back to nature. Even the tourist market is largely of the traditional kind – the stall owners are usually knitting their products in between selling them. Charming lace tablecloths are also on sale.

ⓐ Cape Kaliakra Ⓝ Driving, or booking an organised trip from your resort, is the easiest way to get to Kaliakra. The cape is 12 km (7½ miles) from Kavarna, from where you can take a public bus as far as Balgarevo, which still leaves you with a 6-km (4-mile) walk. Tour companies run buses from Kavarna and Balchik among other places Ⓛ 08.00–18.00 May–Oct ❶ Admission charge, payable at the booth on the approach road

THINGS TO SEE & DO

Muzeum Kaliakra (Kaliakra Museum)

The restaurant area includes the entrance to the small museum. Housed in a cave in the side of the cliff face, it's a charming add-on, right in keeping with the authentic feel of Kaliakra. As you enter, sounds of the sea, birds or battles quietly echo. In two small rooms are housed collections of pottery and jewellery from the medieval, Hellenic and Byzantine periods that give a brief insight into the area's colourful history.

▲ *The dramatic limestone cliffs of Kaliakra*

Nature-spotting

Kaliakra is special mainly for the wildlife that makes its home there. The area is the habitat for over 240 rare and endangered animal and plant species.

TURBULENT TIMES AT THE CAPE

While today Kaliakra has a peace and serenity that provides a counterpoint to the busy seaside resorts, it was not always so tranquil. The setting has seen both warfare and tragic sacrifice in the course of its history and mythology.

The Battle of Cape Kaliakra saw the Russian fleet take on the Turks in 1791. Despite their fewer boats and inferior firepower, the Russians saw off the Ottoman attack and the Turks retreated to Istanbul. It was the last battle in a war that had dragged on for five years.

The most popular legend that has survived, probably because of the picture it paints of the noble Bulgarian character, surrounds the Ottoman Conquest of the 14th century. It is said that, rather than undergo forced conversion to Islam and other humiliations at the hands of the invading Turks, 40 Bulgarian women tied their hair together and jumped into the Black Sea to their deaths from the rocks at Kaliakra. The story is commemorated with an obelisk at the entrance to the site, called the Gate of the 40 Maidens.

It is also said that the cape was formed when St Nicholas, the patron saint of sailors, was attempting to escape the Turks, and God made the land longer and longer to aid his getaway. And a third legend has it that one of Alexander the Great's successors, Lysimachus, also tried to escape to the cape after stealing the royal treasure. Unfortunately for him, the powers above looked less beneficently on his plight and he drowned in a storm.

◓ *The cliffs provided an ideal site for fortifications*

EXPOSURE TO THE ELEMENTS

Kaliakra is an exposed spot, subject to extremes of temperature not felt in the Black Sea coast resorts, and walking around it in inappropriate clothing can be a miserable experience. In the summer there is little shade offering respite from the sun, and sunhats, water and suntan lotion are all advisable. The nature reserve is closed in winter proper, but at the tail end of the season it can already feel a little chilly there, with no protection from the sea winds. Even if it doesn't seem a cold day when you set out, it's worth taking an extra jumper or coat to be sure.

Walking

Kaliakra Nature Reserve is all about getting back to nature, and the main thing to do is walk. Several brief diversions lead off from the main path, often to a clifftop ledge offering a stunning view of the surrounding sea and cliffs.

TAKING A BREAK

Restaurant

If all that sea air and exploring gets you a bit out of breath, the main path eventually brings you to a small restaurant, where you can enjoy a pick-me-up overlooking the waves. ❸ At the museum entrance (see page 69)

Dobrich

A charming town that has truly embraced the café culture of the Mediterranean, Dobrich is a good stop-off point if you're travelling between the coast and the Romanian border, but it merits a visit anyway. Largely untouched by the tourism and property fever that have galvanised the coastal towns, Dobrich's citizens just go nonchalantly

🔺 *Soak up the sunshine in Dobrich town park*

about their business, which seems mostly to be relaxing, eating and drinking. Its main square is peopled with carefree individuals who seem to belie their country's difficult recent history. The vibe is almost studenty: happy-go-lucky and laissez-faire.

Here, tourist kitsch is avoided; the bars, restaurants and clubs do a fine line in casual chic and could hold their own alongside the establishments of Bulgaria's larger resorts and towns. Whether you want to sip a cappuccino while watching the world go by, pose over cocktails with the town's trendy set or dance until daylight, Dobrich has something to suit your leisure needs. And that applies even if you enjoy somewhat unconventional ways of relaxing. In the centre of town, on pl Svoboda, is one of those upward bungee jumps, where you are attached securely to a strong band of elastic and pinged up in the air.

One of the best places to take it easy – which you will certainly want to do if you were brave enough to try the upward bungee jump – is the town park, a beautifully landscaped area that is far bigger than you would expect to find in a relatively small town. It hosts climbing frames for the kids and cafés for the adults, and is perfect for a pleasant stroll.

🔘 The most important of the roads serving Bulgaria's coast pass through Dobrich, which lies 37 km (23 miles) from the Romanian border. From the town, it's a direct drive to the border towns of Kardam and Silistra, and you can also reach Varna and the northern resorts, which makes the town an ideal stopping-off point if you're continuing your journey by car. Trains and buses also serve Dobrich

THINGS TO SEE & DO

Etnografski Muzei (Ethnographical Museum)

Full of farming equipment and traditional costumes, Dobrich's Ethnographical Museum is one of the more engaging of its kind. Unfortunately the opening hours can be a bit erratic, so you may have to just knock at the door and hope somebody answers. The converted black-and-white 19th-century house is striking in itself.

ⓐ Bul 25 Septemvri ⓛ Approximately 09.00–17.00 Mon–Fri; closed for lunch, closed Sat & Sun

Izkustvo Galeria (Art Gallery)

A well-organised collection of paintings, sculpture, graphics and plastic arts, mostly contemporary, but with the odd piece dating back further. The majority of artists whose work is on show are Bulgarian, but there are a few pieces by other Europeans. The gallery hosts occasional opening events and themed collections, mainly grouped by nationality or region. Children's art and photography are two recent examples. The informative website provides a comprehensive list of the exhibitors, works and upcoming events.
ⓐ Balgariya 14 ⓣ 058 602 215 ⓦ www.gallery.dobrich.com
ⓔ gallerydobrich@hotmail.com ⓛ 09.00–12.30 & 13.30–18.00 Mon–Sat, closed Sun ⓘ Admission charge

Muzei Yordan Yovkov (Yordan Yovkov Museum)

Named after one of Bulgaria's most famous 20th-century writers, the museum houses a selection of old pictures and artefacts, including personal belongings, relating to the life of Yovkov and a couple of his contemporaries.
ⓐ Intersection of 25 Septemvri and Otets Paisii, opposite the park
ⓣ 058 662 213 ⓛ 08.00–12.00 & 13.00–17.00 Mon–Fri, closed Sat & Sun
ⓘ Admission charge

Prirodonauchen Muzei (Natural History Museum)

Previously the Regional Museum of History, this place currently features a display on natural history while the old history section is revamped. The historical section is set to open again in 2007.
ⓐ In the park, just off Otets Paisii ⓛ 09.00–17.00 Mon–Sat; closed Sun, except by appointment ⓘ Admission charge

Stariyat Dobrich (Old Dobrich)

Dobrich was once a famous arts and crafts centre, and this period of its history is commemorated in the old quarter, where pottery, jewellery and woodcarvings are among the souvenirs made and sold in various workshops.

ⓐ Bul 25 Septemvri 37 ⓣ 058 29307 ⓛ 08.00–18.00 (summer); 08.00–17.00 (winter)

TAKING A BREAK

Bars & cafés

Blaga Vaize ££ Smart café and terrace overlooking the town's main square, serving a wide range of coffees. ⓐ Corner of Balgariya and bul 25 Septemvri ⓣ 058 60 14 75 ⓛ 08.00–23.00

Cadife ££ The owner of this trendy lounge café-bar has a sense of humour, if the places of honour at the bar reserved for Michael Jordan and Beyoncé are anything to go by. ⓐ Bul 25 Septemvri ⓛ 07.00–23.00

AFTER DARK

Bacardi Club ££ Fashionable nightspot catering to the city's chic set, who are entertained by a range of top DJs. Coolly done out with an outside bar and terrace covered by cream canopies, the interior is equally smart. No main meals, but you can munch on sandwiches or desserts while listening to dance hits. It's right next to a children's play area, so if you're going in the daytime the kids will be entertained too.

ⓐ Opposite the Yordan Yakob Museum ⓣ 0885 63 95 66 ⓛ 08.00–04.00

Sezoni ££ Smart restaurant of a quality far higher than you would expect in a small Bulgarian town. The surroundings are bright, clean and cheerful, the staff friendly and the food enjoyable. Choose from a range of pizza, pasta, standard meat grills and cakes and desserts. The website has no English translation but includes pictures and prices for the food.

ⓐ Balgariya 4 ⓣ 058 60 16 06 ⓦ www.sezoni.dobrich.com ⓔ office@sezoni.dobrich.com ⓛ 07.00–23.00

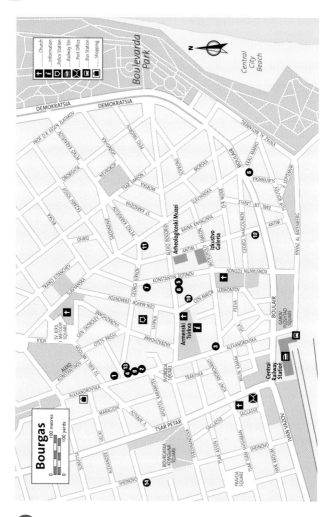

Bourgas

Church
Information
Police Station
Railway Stn
Post Office
Bus Station
Shopping

Excursions in the south

Bourgas

Wandering around central Bourgas – and wandering is the pace of life here – you'll feel more like you're in a Mediterranean town than a former Communist city. The old man who plays music from *The Godfather* on his accordion in the public park only reinforces the feeling of being in a sunny Italian piazza. The park is the town's centrepiece – it has neat gardens with statues and benches. Cultural and leisure facilities are everywhere, from the museums, theatres, galleries and art shops to the many cafés and restaurants along and around the central pedestrianised area, ul Aleksandrovska. Indeed, judging by the businesses in the city centre, Bourgas citizens seem to have little to do other than sip coffee and tuck into indulgent ice cream and cakes, then walk off all the excess calories through a stroll and a chat with a friend. The town is in fact the fourth biggest in Bulgaria, and the country's largest port, but you would not know this from its calm vibe.

As such, it's a relaxing spot to while away a few hours, and makes an urbane change from the beach holiday atmosphere of the coastal towns. It also has a sophisticated nightlife ranging from piano bars to trendy clubs. While it is not as cosmopolitan as Varna, it is the central hub of the southern strip of resorts, and if you're heading south you will almost certainly pass through it. Although it might not be on your list of must-sees for the coast, the leisurely atmosphere really has something going for it, and if you stop off for lunch you will probably find yourself wanting to stick around a bit longer and enjoy the social scene. Bourgas is also home to some of the most interesting lakes in the area, which are a magnet to bird-watchers, nature lovers in general and anyone who just enjoys an unspoiled view.

Ⓝ Bourgas is a main hub on the coastal road. It has its own airport, from where you can take the number 15 bus into town. It will leave you in the centre, close to the train and bus stations. The Bourgas Lakes lie north, west and south of the town itself. A bus will take you very close to the

⬥ *Flanked by a weeping willow, the peaceful Armenian Church*

conservation centre, to the left of the E87 as you go south from Bourgas, although if you want to cover a lot of ground, going by car would be better.

BEACHES

With Bourgas having such a lively centre and social life, sometimes it's easy to forget it's also a coastal town. The beach is within easy reach of the centre, and has some sea gardens running alongside it, home to the city's open-air theatre. It's clean, patrolled by lifeguards, access is free, and there tend to be fewer people here than in the resorts. It doesn't have the range of activities of the more tourist-oriented towns, but volleyball and windsurfing are available and there's a smattering of restaurants if you don't want to walk back into town to eat.

THINGS TO SEE & DO

Arheologiceski Muzei (Archaeological Museum)
Statues, coins, jewellery and ceramics plus a popular natural history feature.
ⓐ Ul Aleko Bogoridi 21 ① 056 84 35 41 Ⓦ www.burgasmuseums.bg (for all city museums) ① 09.00–18.00 Mon–Sat, closed Sun (summer); 08.00–17.00 Mon–Fri, closed Sat & Sun (winter)

Armenski Tsirkva (Armenian Church)
The small Armenian Church is something a little different from the usual religious buildings in the region. With a weeping willow outside, and opposite a small park, it is in a picturesquely quiet location. Inside it's atmospheric, with lights and pictures and a lot more colour than you might be used to seeing in church.
ⓐ Bul Aleko Bogoridi, near Hotel Bulgaria

Izkustvo Galeria (Art Gallery)
Housed in a 100-year-old former synagogue, the gallery houses over 2,500 paintings, drawings and sculptures – mostly religious scenes and land- and seascapes from the local area.

 Mitropolit Simeon 24  www.bourgas.net/local/ArtGallery
 056 842 169  Admission charge

TAKING A BREAK

Unison Café ££ ❶   Serves salads, snacks, and a range of alcoholic and non-alcoholic cocktails. Desserts and mousses rotate temptingly in a display cabinet.  Ul Aleksandrovska 67  056 82 52 52

AFTER DARK

Restaurants
Amstel Restaurant ££ ❷   Three-storey restaurant serving Bulgarian and international dishes, mainly meat and fish, plus desserts. A warm atmosphere that's reminiscent of an upmarket northern European pub.  Ul Aleksandrovska 49  056 82 76 29  10.00–02.00

Bulgaria ££ ❸   As the name suggests, this place serves up the national cuisine alongside European dishes. The romantic feel of the restaurant is supported by live piano music.  Ul Aleksandrovska 21  056 87 52 05  www.bulgaria-hotel.com  hotelbulgaria@bginfo.net  07.00–23.00

Europa ££ ❹   Unpretentious eatery offering Italian-style pizza, plus other local and European meals. If you're lucky there might be some live music too.  Ul Aleksandrovska 59  056 82 88 45  10.00–01.00  Cash only

Maracas Pub and Pizza ££ ❺   A light and airy eatery dotted with plants – the ideal alternative if you've had enough of traditional Bulgarian joints with the dark, wooden interiors. Italian favourites pizza and pasta are on offer, plus BBQ, salads and meat dishes with a range of vegetarian options.  Ul Aleko Bogoridi 19  07.00–24.00

⬥ There's a great range of bars and cafés in Bourgas

Talasacra ££ ❻ Bright and cheerful restaurant that puts on live music to go with its tasty Bulgarian and Serbian grill. ⓐ Ul Boulair 37 ⓣ 056 84 37 17 ⓔ in_house@abv.bg ⓛ 09.00–24.00

Zhelezniat Svetilnik ££ ❼ Traditional Bulgarian hospitality, folk music and food. In summer they do a BBQ outside. Choose from over 200 wines to accompany your meal. ⓐ Ul Konstantin Fotinov 28 ⓣ 056 84 18 19 ⓛ 10.00–24.00 ⓘ Cash only

Atagen £££ ❽ Chic, modern black-and-white restaurant, ideal for any smart occasion. Fresh ingredients served in international dishes. ⓐ Bul San Stefano 129 ⓣ 056 81 22 18 ⓔ restaurant@atagen91.com ⓛ 08.00–24.00

Bars & clubs

Bacardi Café-Club ££ ❾ The hangout of Bourgas's fashionable set, this is the place to recline on a leopard print chair over cakes and cocktails. Two levels play commercial dance music to the in-crowd. ⓐ Ul Aleksandrovska 51 ⓣ 056 82 76 29 ⓛ 07.00–02.00 ⓘ Cash only

Fifth Avenue Piano Bar ££ ❿ Dimly lit and very plush venue with live music every night at 22.00. ⓐ Opposite the Armenian Church ⓛ 21.00–05.00

Grolsch Beer House ££ ⓫ Large British-style pub, also serving a range of national cuisine, in particular fish dishes. Has another outlet at the Sea Gardens. ⓐ Ul Raina Knyaginya ⓣ 0897 23 23 17 ⓛ 10.00–01.00 ⓘ Cash only

Groovy Bar ££ ⓬ Whether you want Cuban music and salsa dancing, funky 1970s disco, blues, soul or simply a game of pool or darts, this down-to-earth place has got it. ⓐ Ul Antim I 10 ⓣ 0886 65 80 57 ⓦ www.groovybar.com ⓛ 24 hours ⓘ Cash only

🔺 *There's a Mediterranean air about the town*

Kadiffe Café-Piano Bar ££ ⓭ Classy interior and terrace that plays a wide range of music, with pop, retro Latino and Bulgarian tunes, as well as live performances at the stylish grand piano. ⓐ Ul Aleksandrovska 61 ⓣ 056 84 28 56 ⓛ 24 hours ⓘ Cash only

Karaoke Bar ££ ⓮ You might not be quite as talented as the stars whose photos line the wall, such as Jimi Hendrix, but a willingness to have a go is all that's required here. ⓐ Ul Kliment Ohridski ⓣ 056 84 16 37 ⓛ 20.00–04.00

Bourgas Lakes

Bird lovers should not come to the Black Sea coast without taking advantage of the many opportunities to do a little bird spotting. And there are few places richer in species than the Bourgas Lakes, which host 316 out of the country's total of around 400. Fourteen of them, including the Dalmatian pelican and pygmy cormorant, are globally endangered. The site is on the migratory route, the Via Pontica, and it's possible to spot some of the thousands of storks, raptors and pelicans who fly over it each year on their long commute. If you have the good luck and good timing to stop by at peak migration time, the spectacular image of huge flocks of birds taking flight cannot fail to move you. Take your camera and be quick on the button.

Endangered plants, fish and mammals also take refuge here, with much of the 9,500 hectares (23,480 acres) either already, or likely to be, categorised as a protected area. The lakes, Atanasovo, Bourgas, Mandresko, Poda and Pomorie, are also a source of sea salt, and mud from them is used in various holistic treatments. The very brave can even take the plunge into the mud at its source. In fact there are opportunities for swimming throughout the area, provided the weather allows, and you may also go fishing.

While the site is a twitcher's paradise, like Srebarna, it can also be enjoyed by the layman with little interest in spotting rare species. The

⬥ *Bird lovers should head to the Bourgas Lakes*

Bourgas Lakes have a scenic value of their own. The various combinations of reeds, fields and water provide many photo opportunities, and if you manage to catch a sunset or sunrise you will get some classic snaps to take home.

Getting to, and around, the lakes is not easy, and you are required to stick to the permitted pathways. Probably the most enjoyable way to try is by boat trip, which can be arranged by the Poda Information and Visitors' Centre ☎ 056 85 05 40 ✉ bspbpoda@mobikom.com. The centre will also lend you binoculars and has telescopes on the site. The staff will point out whichever birds are within viewing distance 🄽 Buses stop within 400 m (440 yds) of the visitor's centre.

Strandzha (Strandja) National Park

The Strandzha mountain range extends through the European part of Turkey and southern Bulgaria. The national park is the country's largest protected area, making up 1 per cent of the country's territory, and 50 per cent of its flora can be found in the park. It's a varied and beautiful landscape of mountain peaks, valleys, rivers and forest, and part of the park has the distinction of being one of Bulgaria's sunniest places. The rivers that run through the area are said to be so clean and full of fish that you can catch your supper by hand, and the locals see the water as holy, with curative powers. Whether or not you believe them, the fresh air and openness of Strandzha will certainly do your constitution some good.

But more than its nature and plant life, Strandzha is interesting for the culture that has been preserved there. Its traditional villages are worth a visit both for the charming wooden cottages that seem to be straight from another century and also for the customs that have survived alongside them. Perhaps the most intriguing of these is fire dancing, when young villagers fast all day before going into a trance and moving quickly over hot embers. It might not please the health and safety inspectors, but thousands of onlookers make the journey to the

◆ *The forests of Strandzha*

village of Balgari to witness the annual event (see page 106). There are many other fairs and saints' days celebrated, and it's worth checking ahead to see if you can catch something.

On top of the cultural possibilities, there is a range of physical activities available, though it is safe to say you won't be disturbed by the shrieks of extreme sports practitioners. The pursuits are of a more gentle nature: as well as a spot of fishing, you can also hire a bicycle and explore the area on two wheels, or even go trekking. Bird-watchers also make a point of visiting the park, particularly at the very beginning and tail end of the summer season.

ⓐ Strandzha National Park Administration, Malko Tarnovo

ⓣ 0888 51 39 67 ⓔ info@discoverstrandja.com ⓝ If you're intending to stay a while or want to find out more details, head for the Strandzha National Park Administration at Malko Tarnovo, just a few miles from the Turkish border. If you're coming via the coast road, turn off at Tsarevo. You can also reach the town from Bourgas via car or the infrequent bus service, but be warned that the road is in poor condition (at least two buses go from Bourgas's central bus station to the main villages in the Strandzha Park every day)

> **TIP**
> Take your passport. Strandzha National Park is deep in southern Bulgaria, and, even though you don't get particularly close to the Turkish border, the area is considered a border zone, and you may well be stopped at one of the various checkpoints and asked for your papers.

● *Life revolves around the sea in Bulgaria*

Food & drink

Bulgarian cuisine tends to be dominated by meat. Grilled pork, chicken and beef are the staples that can be found on most menus. A standard meal in an average restaurant would consist of meat served with potatoes in some form and a portion or two of vegetables.

In this part of the world, many people still find the idea of anyone voluntarily going without meat a strange one. This is despite the fact that the country's varied geography and temperate climate result in a superb selection of vegetables, grown traditionally in the countryside. Much of this produce is organic – not that the Bulgarians would use that word to describe it. Here, it's just how they come. Cabbage, peppers, aubergines, garlic and onions are among the most common vegetables. Typical accompaniments are soups before the main course and salads with it, and you will almost always be brought bread as well.

Yoghurt with everything is another theme. Sometimes it seems that there is virtually no dish that yoghurt cannot accompany, and many Bulgarians eat it every day of their lives. You will almost certainly have the opportunity to try the plain kind, usually made from cow's milk, during your stay.

The food reflects the country's politics and history. You'll be able to spot Turkish, Greek and Middle Eastern influences. But the cuisine has also been shaped by the West. Many meals do not differ significantly from standard European fare, and pizza and pasta are now infiltrating the restaurants, especially in the larger towns and resorts that see the greatest numbers of foreign tourists.

This is particularly true on the Black Sea coast. Natural entrepreneurs, the Bulgarians have responded to the tastes of their visitors, and it's impossible to walk for more than a few minutes in some resorts without seeing the offer of a full English breakfast chalked onto a blackboard. Jacket potatoes, Sunday roasts, steak specials, omelettes – all are standard in the tourist areas, which means that if you're travelling with your family you're unlikely to have to worry about what the kids are going to eat. Another popular branch of cuisine is Bulgarian recipes, but cooked in a Western way to make them more palatable to foreign tastebuds. This usually means less stodgily.

Some restaurants, particularly in Varna, which is increasingly catering to a business and investor crowd as well as locals and tourists, have gone a step further and put together a truly first-class international dining experience. For the cost of a mediocre meal in your home country, here you can experience the highest standards in food and service, and it's worth spending the money on at least one such evening out during your stay.

But the Black Sea coast's main cuisine highlight is the fish. Many restaurants are on or right next to the beach, and the comprehensive list of delicacies will be served as fresh as it's possible to get. Some places even have tanks of live catch on the premises, ready and waiting for your selection. Bluefish, sea bass, calamari, salmon, swordfish, wolf fish, dorade, shrimps, herring, crab, shark, scad, crayfish, octopus, mussels – if it swims in the Black Sea, you can usually dine on it in one of the coastal restaurants.

No discussion of Bulgarian cuisine would be complete without reference to wine. The climate and geography, plus a long tradition of winemaking, have earned the local wine a high reputation abroad. The country is revered in particular for its reds, which are fantastic value and of very high quality. On the Black Sea coast, however, the long, mild winters provide favourable conditions for white wine production, and over half of the country's whites come from this area. Merlot, Cabernet Sauvignon, Sauvignon Blanc and Chardonnay are among the many grape varieties on offer. Annoyingly, customs laws restrict the amount of wine you can take out of the country, because at the prices charged you may be tempted to take home a whole case. Nonetheless, that is no reason not to drink a lot of the stuff while you're there. In restaurants, it is almost always possible to order by the glass. The big cities have specialist wine shops if you want to take home something really special, but you won't have to dig too deeply in your pocket to buy quality.

A colourful pub in Varna

Spirits too have something of a tradition in Bulgaria. *Mastika*, an anise-flavoured liqueur of 45 per cent alcohol, and *rakia*, a 40 per cent proof brandy commonly made from plums, apricots or grapes, are often available on restaurant menus. But be warned – they are not for the faint-hearted. As for soft drinks, the usual range of fizzy stuff is available, as are juices, though it's worth checking before you order whether they are fresh or from a bottle or carton if you have a preference. While the tap water is safe to drink, the low price of the bottled variety means that few people choose that option.

On the Black Sea coast, you will seldom find restaurants that limit themselves to offering evening entrées, and while cafés that only serve coffee and snacks are slightly more common, it is not the rule. The majority of eateries are a combination of café, restaurant and sometimes bar. They open early in the morning to serve coffee and breakfast, typically including English fry-ups and omelettes; in the afternoon they might offer sandwiches and salad. They will also present a range of main meals, such as pizza, meat and fish dishes, which are mainly taken in the evening, when they serve until 23.00 or so, although it can be later in the larger resorts. This results in large menus that are available all day, so it should rarely be a problem to get what you want to eat, when and where you want it.

In Varna and other large towns, the more upmarket restaurants do accept credit cards, but this is not yet the norm and it's a good idea to take cash with you just in case. Service is usually friendly and professional, and in all but the smallest, local establishments your waiter or waitress will speak at least some English. Until a few years ago, tipping was unheard of, but now it is appropriate to leave around 10 per cent, slightly more if the meal or service was exceptional. Provided you do a bit of research you should find many great places to eat – many holidaymakers have extremely happy memories of meals on the Black Sea coast – that will leave you with plenty of change.

Menu decoder

Menus will almost always have an English, and sometimes German, translation, but if you intend to spend any amount of time in Bulgaria it can be worth making the effort to learn some of the basic food terminology. Listed below (in Roman script) are some of the traditional dishes that you might come across.

Banitsa Traditional oven-baked pastry with cheese, eggs or vegetables, in which – on special occasions – lucky charms are put

Bob Bean soup with herbs, tomatoes and onion

Cheverme Chunks of lamb, spiced and stuffed, and roasted on a spit

Chushki byurek Peppers stuffed with egg, cheese and herbs and fried in breadcrumbs

Gyuvetch The name is a type of pot, in which is served a vegetable and meat dish

Kashkaval pane Cheese fried in breadcrumbs

Kavarma A stew made up of spicy pieces of beef, pork or chicken with leeks or onions and red pepper. It can also be served on a skewer

Kebapcheta Spicy homemade pork or veal sausages cooked on the grill

Kufteta Spicy meatballs or hamburgers mixed with breadcrumbs

Meshana skara Mixed grill

Panagyurishte eggs Poached eggs and yoghurt

Plakiya Slow cooked fish stew

Pulneni Chushkis Meso Oven baked peppers stuffed with pork or beef, rice and vegetables

Riba Plakiya Carp covered in lemon and sautéed in garlic, oil, tomato paste and herbs

Ribnik Fish pie, usually carp, with rice

Sarmi Minced meat with rice, onion and seasoning wrapped in cabbage leaves or similar

Shashlik A type of kebab with skewered meat and vegetables, which can include onions, mushrooms and peppers

Shopska salad Tomatoes, cucumbers, peppers, onions, cheese and parsley

Sirene po shopski Feta cheese with chopped tomatoes, egg, peppers and herbs cooked in a pot

Snazhanka salad Yoghurt, cucumber, pickles, garlic and walnuts with seasoning

Supa topcheta Meatball soup with rice and a range of vegetables and herbs

Tarator Cold soup containing yoghurt, cucumber, garlic and nuts and seasoned with herbs, traditionally eaten in the summer

Below are some more general words and expressions:

Bira Beer
Chai Tea
Desert Dessert
Hliab Bread
Izvinete, kade e toaletnata? Excuse me, where is the toilet?
Kafe Coffee
Kartof Potato
Meso Meat
Na Zdrave! Cheers!
Napitka Drink
Obiad Lunch
Otset Vinegar
Parjeni kartofi Chips
Parjola Steak
Pileshko Poultry
Piper Pepper
Plot Fruit
Rezervacia Reservation
Riba Fish

Salata Salad
Sandvich Sandwich
Sladolet Ice cream
Smetkata, molia!/Ako obichate, mojeli smetkata? Can I have the bill, please?
Sok Juice
Sol Salt
Svinsko Pork
Teleshko Beef
Toaletni Toilet
Vecheria Dinner
Vegetarianets (male) Vegetarian
Vegetarianka (female) Vegetarian
Vino Wine
Voda Water
Zahar Sugar
Zakuska Breakfast
Zelenchuk Vegetable

Shopping

Bulgarians are natural and enthusiastic shoppers, and visitors will find no shortage of their preferred merchandise, be it locally handmade souvenirs or designer fashion. A plethora of clothes and cosmetics stores reflect Bulgarian women's attention to their appearance, and some visitors advise travelling to the area with an empty suitcase that can be filled up with bargains before the return journey. Prices of many items are far lower than in Western countries, and, provided you avoid the boutiques that sell top-of-the-range imported designer gear, a shopping spree will not deplete your holiday funds too drastically. While the smaller villages have a more limited range of shops and stalls, finding the goods you are after should be no problem in the larger resorts.

WHERE TO SHOP

Varna is the undoubted shopping capital of the Black Sea coast – with its unashamed love of consumerism it is hard to imagine that the city was under the Communist regime as recently as 1989. The majority of high-end shops are concentrated in the pedestrianised area around pl Nezavisimost, Bul Knyaz Boris I and ul Preslav, where the stores rival anything Sofia has on offer. Familiar high-street names such as Benetton and Mango sit alongside designer boutiques. Bulgarians seem to be particularly into accessorising, with shoe shops, jewellers, leather goods stores and underwear outlets all ubiquitous.

DESIGNER GOODS

At the high end of the market, while there are bargains to be found, prices tend to be comparable to those in Western stores, and you are unlikely to make much of a saving if you buy official designer goods in Bulgaria rather than at home. If you do spot big-name labels at dramatically reduced prices, you are probably looking at a well-made copy. You'll find upmarket clothes and cosmetics stores anywhere that sees a large number of tourists. Prices tend to be higher outside the main resorts, so the better deals on the Black Sea coast are likely to be in

Varna. For prices, this rule holds in general: if something is imported, as most genuine designer goods are, expect to pay the same as you would elsewhere.

MARKETS

While the upper end of the market may not offer significant reductions, there are plenty of locally made bargains to be had elsewhere, such as in the many markets to be found both in major cities and in the smaller villages. The joy of such places is not only the low-cost items you can pick up, but also seeing your goods made on the spot, often by old women using techniques and materials that have been passed down over generations. One of the best places for this is right outside Varna's Cathedral of the Assumption, where the cheerful women chatting and knitting outside create a relaxed atmosphere, contrasting with the pomp and formality inside.

The kind of market where your purchase is woven or made before your eyes is just one branch of Bulgarian street trading, however. Also on sale from stalls is a wealth of goods that you might find in markets back home, but for a fraction of the price. Places like Sunny Beach are full of stalls selling sunglasses, leather wallets, clothes and belts. There is often a British flavour to the goods on sale, such as football shirts with Wayne Rooney's name printed on the back and pink and white tracksuit tops emblazoned with the name Victoria Beckham. If you want a more permanent souvenir of your holiday, there are plenty of tattoo and piercing parlours among the clothes stalls. Seaside wares also form a big part of the goods on offer, from flip-flops, swimsuits and beach towels to lilos and other inflatables, plus equipment for the various watersports on offer.

Fruit and vegetable markets also yield their fair share of bargains, and even the food on sale in local shops and supermarkets will seem superb value to the Westerner.

HANDICRAFTS

As well as lace and knitted goods, Bulgaria is also known for its ceramics, wood carvings and carpets. There are traces of Soviet influence, but with

a new twist, such as the Russian dolls on sale in the flea market over the road from Varna's cathedral, where traditional kinds sit alongside versions of George Bush and Vladimir Putin. Bulgaria is a religious country, and Orthodox iconography is also commonly on sale, in particular near the churches popular with tourists. Other types of art also make a good souvenir of your trip. Varna's main art gallery hosts guest exhibitions from which you can purchase works, and you'll also find specialised art shops in the larger resorts.

Another of Bulgaria's fortes is its wine (see page 93). The country's geographical position and Mediterranean climate mean it is a major wine producer and exporter. Sadly you are limited to taking only two litres out of the country, as the price to quality ratio is excellent. However, that does not stop wine lovers buying and consuming it before leaving the country! Bulgaria's red wine has a particularly high reputation.

HAGGLING

While haggling used to be common throughout the Balkans, Bulgaria's Black Sea coast is getting increasingly Westernised, and the practice is no longer appropriate at many of the outlets in the area. However, some tourists find that at some of the less formal market stalls it is worth trying to negotiate a discount, particularly for copies of designer goods or if you're buying several things. Use your judgement.

Children

Bulgarians love children and they will be welcome in hotels and restaurants up and down the coast. It might not be the obvious place to go with the kids, but in fact there is a lot on offer for younger visitors and many advantages to a family beach holiday on the Black Sea coast rather

○ *Big wheel and small train at Golden Sands*

than, say, the more obvious resorts in Spain, Portugal or Greece. Firstly, the low cost of accommodation and dining out means that you can bring a large family here for far less than it would cost to have a similar holiday further west, meaning more money for entertaining.

And there is plenty of that for children. The main resorts have lots of children's activities on offer and you will rarely drive far along the coast road before passing an aquatic park with a tangle of water chutes and slides. Dodgems, go-karting and mini-golf are to be found in some resorts, and you can also hire bikes and scooters. The larger hotels also run various programmes of traditional sports for kids including tennis and football. Then, of course, there are the various watersports on offer. Safety standards have improved dramatically, but of course it is always advisable to book with a reputable company or through your hotel. Children's playgrounds are a common site wherever you go in the area and Golden Sands even has a large Ferris wheel on the beachfront. Varna's Dolphinarium (see page 35) is great entertainment for kids.

One of the highlights of beach holidays for children is swimming in the sea. In general, the sea in this area does not suffer from strong tides and is usually calm. A flag system sometimes indicates where swimming is safe and a lifeguard is in attendance. Bigger resorts like Sunny Beach also have children's pools.

Unlike in some foreign resorts, food should not be a problem, even for fussy eaters. The national cuisine is not too dissimilar to the standard international dishes that children enjoy, and even in restaurants that cater mainly to locals, you're unlikely to encounter anything too spicy or off-putting. In the larger resorts, the menus are typically designed with the British diner in mind. Pizza, pasta, chips, salads and omelettes are ubiquitous and some restaurants even have special children's menus.

Cheap soft toys can usually be picked up in the seaside markets, plus the usual beachfront paraphernalia such as buckets and spades and pool inflatables. All in all, there is enough to keep the kids fed and entertained, without having to splash out too much to do so.

Sports & activities

First on the must-do list for visitors to Bulgaria's Black Sea coast is usually watersports. Just as the country's ski resorts have upped their game and now represent a competitive alternative to the slopes of Western Europe, so too have Black Sea coast entrepreneurs put together a package of seaside activities that will tire out even the most zealous adrenalin junkies. Water-skiing, parachuting, paragliding, hang-gliding, surfing, scuba-diving, yachting, or hiring paddle boats and rowing boats, are just some of the options. Albena, Sunny Beach and Golden Sands probably have the most comprehensive range, but even the smaller towns usually offer one or two such activities. Some have a diving centre. It's quite easy to find somewhere to take your PADI certificate should you wish.

The cheap petrol prices mean that whatever sport you fancy, it's not going to deplete your holiday funds too much to do it. Safety standards are generally very high, but of course you should use a reputable firm – your hotel will probably be able to recommend one. Swimming is usually possible as the waters are mainly calm and shallow. The larger resorts also have pools and there are several water parks dotted along the coast. You can also find the usual sports away from the water – tennis, football and mini-golf are fairly common and some places organise sports tournaments.

Bird-watching is another draw. The Bourgas Lakes, Pomorie, Cape Kaliakra and Lake Srebarna are among the best sites for twitchers. If you're planning to come especially for the birdlife, May to June and September to the middle of October are probably your best bet, but there will be something to see whenever you're here. See page 68 for some advice on getting started.

Birds are partly attracted to the coastal area's wide open spaces, and hikers too will see the allure. There are some great walks to do, particularly at Strandzha National Park and Srebarna. Local tourist and information offices or museums can often suggest routes.

But if all of the above sounds too much like hard work, the coast also has more relaxing pursuits on offer. Some of the mud from the area is used in alternative health treatments, and many resorts have spa centres offering everything from a soothing massage to anti-ageing therapy.

● *Try windsurfing at Sunny Beach*

LIFESTYLE

Festivals & events

EVENTS ON THE BLACK SEA COAST

Discovery

Bulgaria's answer to the Eurovision Song Contest takes place in May.
Cheesy fun as composers and singers from around the world make their
way to Varna to take part in a pop competition. The music is matched by
an array of imaginative costumes and performances.

Ⓦ www.discoveryfest.com Ⓔ festival@discoveryfest.com

Fire dancing at Balgari

The first weekend in June, or around that time, sees a traditional fire-
dancing display in the village of Balgari, in Strandzha National Park.
Sacrificial sheep and a religious parade form part of the ritual, which
involves young participants dressed in white moving quickly over hot
embers.

Varna Summer International Music Festival

The oldest music festival in Bulgaria has now been running for 80 years.
Throughout June and July, Bulgarian and foreign performers stage
music, theatre and ballet shows.

Ⓣ 052 65 91 23 Ⓦ www.varnasummerfest.org Ⓔ varna_culture@varna.bg

Varna Summer International Jazz Festival

Hosted by the Archaeological Museum, the city's much respected jazz
festival runs in August. In the past it has featured musicians from
Central and Eastern Europe plus France and the US.

Ⓣ 052 30 23 22 Ⓦ www.vsjf.com

International Festival of Folk Music in Bourgas

Up and running for over four decades, Bourgas hosts concerts, a scientific
conference, handicraft expo, plus workshops and film and photographic
activities in late August.

Varna International Film Festival

Taking place at the end of August or beginning of September, the festival is open to new films that have not been broadcast in the country or won prizes at other festivals.

📧 agrozev@techno-link.com

Apollonia Festival of Arts

Veteran and up-and-coming Bulgarian performers put on concerts, plays, art and photo exhibitions, literary and film events and workshops and master classes in Sozopol, in early September.

🌐 www.apollonia.bg/index.php?lang=en

🔺 *Dancers in traditional dress*

International Short Film Festival

In September, students are given the task of shooting a short film in 48 hours based on two key words. Participants from around the world make their way to Balchik for the event.

Orthodox and Muslim festivals

On top of the national holidays there are various religious occasions, including Orthodox Christian saints' days and Islamic festivities. The precise timing varies from year to year based on the lunar calendar.

PUBLIC HOLIDAYS

New Year's Day 1 January

Viticulturists' Day 14 February – Related to Dionysus, the god of wine and merriment

National Day, also known as **Liberation Day** 3 March – Celebrates the country's liberation from Ottoman rule in 1878

Easter March/April

Labour Day 1 May

St George's Day, also known as **Day of the Bulgarian Army** 6 May

St Cyril and Methodius Day, or **Day of Culture and Literacy** 24 May – Schools are decorated with flowers in honour of the brothers who devised the Cyrillic alphabet

The Unification of Bulgaria 6 September – A celebration of the return of southern Bulgaria from Ottoman control

Independence Day 22 September – Honouring the country's independence from the Ottoman Empire, achieved in 1908

Day of the Bulgarian Revival Leaders 1 November

Christmas 24–26 December

New Year's Eve 31 December

◉ *Take in the sights from a bus*

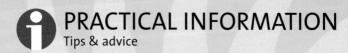

PRACTICAL INFORMATION
Tips & advice

Preparing to go

GETTING THERE

Soaring interest in second homes in Bulgaria – especially from Brits –
means that getting there is far easier and cheaper than it used to
be. Unless you're visiting the country's coastline as part of a bigger
trip around Eastern Europe, flying is your best bet. From the UK or
the rest of Western Europe, the trip is do-able by train or bus, but it's
likely to take over two days and cash savings will be negligible. Direct
flights from the UK to Bulgaria are available with British Airways,
Bulgaria Air and Wizz Air for below £100, although prices do tend to
shoot up in high season.

While Varna and Bourgas both have their own airports, Sofia is better
served, particularly out of season. From the capital, you can take a bus or
train out to the coastal resorts. But with journey times of up to eight
hours, some tourists go for the pricier option of an internal flight from
Sofia to one of the seaside towns.

Another option is to go with a travel operator. Package deals to
Bulgaria have soared in popularity in recent years and most of the main
operators offer good-value holidays, which can often work out cheaper
than doing it independently, although of course you sacrifice some
flexibility. It's worth doing your research before you book. The hotel
rating system is not reliable on the Black Sea coast, with even some
5-star facilities falling well below expectations, so read reviews from
other guests before you commit to a hotel.

Many people are aware that air travel emits CO_2, which contributes
to climate change. You may be interested in the possibility of lessening
the environmental impact of your flight through the charity Climate
Care, which offsets your CO_2 by funding environmental projects around
the world. Visit Ⓦ www.climatecare.org

TOURISM AUTHORITY

Further information, including tourist material, is available from the
Bulgarian Embassy ⓐ 186–188 Queen's Gate, London SW7 5HL, UK

📞 020 7584 9400 or 9433 🌐 www.bulgarianembassy.org.uk
🕐 09.00–18.00 Mon–Fri; closed Sat & Sun

BEFORE YOU LEAVE

No jabs are required before travelling to Bulgaria, although embassies and some other authorities recommend immunisation against hepatitis A, diphtheria, tetanus, typhoid and tuberculosis.

While many people still imagine Bulgaria as a post-Communist society that lacks the basic goods and services we take for granted, those days are long gone – you should be able to pick up everything you need while there. However, if you are going to be staying in one of the smaller resorts, or have a particular favourite brand of something, it might be worth bringing a few supplies with you.

ENTRY FORMALITIES

At the time of writing, Bulgaria is due to join the European Union, which should reduce the red tape surrounding visas. As things stand, EU citizens, including those from Britain and Ireland, the USA, Canada, Australia and New Zealand can all spend up to 90 days in the country without a visa. South African visitors, on the other hand, do need a visa, for which their passport must have six months' validity when they enter the country, as well as blank pages in it. The application procedure takes up to ten working days.

All foreign nationals are required by Bulgarian law to register the address where they are staying at the local police station within two days. Your hotel will take care of this. If you're bringing your car into the country, you must carry proof of ownership.

Custom law places some limits on alcohol (three to four litres of wine and spirits) and cigarettes (200). The restrictions are rather complicated – they are slashed, for example, if you enter the country twice within a month. For a comprehensive list, consult the Bulgarian Embassy website 🌐 www.bulgarianembassy.org.uk

❗ When you leave the country, you are required by law to show a receipt from the hotel where you stayed. If you go on a package holiday, your rep will deal with this. Independent travellers must retain their hotel receipts, which should be issued at the reception desk automatically, although the border official may not necessarily ask you for them.

◆ The station at Bourgas

MONEY

The Bulgarian currency is the lev, or leva in the plural, which is subdivided into 100 stotinki. Both notes and coins come mainly in denominations of 50, 20, 10, 5, 2 and 1. There are almost two leva to the euro. In the main resorts, traveller's cheques should generally be accepted (although you may find yourself paying a small commission), and you should find an ATM fairly easily. Although the better hotels and restaurants are slowly starting to take credit cards, outside of Varna it is better not to assume they will and to carry cash with you just in case.

While banks close at 16.00, bureaux de change are open for an hour or two later, and in the resorts you will find flexible opening hours and occasionally 24-hour outlets. Make sure you check carefully whether the teller intends to charge you commission, as this is now illegal. Some hotels will also change your money for local currency, but check the rate they offer – while some hotels offer a fair figure, many do not. Changing money on the black market is not advisable.

CLIMATE

Bulgaria's Black Sea coast is blessed with something most of us have wished for – a climate that stays mild all year round. Between May and October, the tourist season, the temperature is on average 16°C (60°F) or above. The hottest months are July and August, when average temperatures reach a pleasant, but not sweltering, 23–24°C (74–75°F). The Mediterranean conditions can occasionally be punctuated by winds or a brief spell of heavy rain, but as a rule wet days are few.

BAGGAGE ALLOWANCE

Your baggage allowance will vary depending on the airline you are flying with. British Airways, for example, is likely to let you check in more luggage than the budget airline Wizz Air, and charter flights also tend to have more restrictive baggage allowances. Hand luggage guidelines have altered recently following security alerts. The best idea is to give your airline a call, or check its website, before you fly to find out what the current restrictions are.

During your stay

AIRPORTS

Having struggled to keep up with expanding traffic, Sofia airport is currently undergoing renovation. If you fly into the capital, you can pick up the 84 bus, which departs every 15 or 20 minutes or so into the city centre. Buy your ticket beforehand. The number 30 minibus also makes the journey. Both run between 07.00 and 23.00. As is the case to some extent throughout the country, if you take a taxi you run the risk of being overcharged, although if you find an honest driver the fare will usually be very reasonable, particularly if you are in a group. If you're planning to drive on to the coast, several major car hire companies have an office in the airport arrivals hall. If you need to contact the airport, call ℹ 052 57 33 23.

From Sofia, you can take a flight to the Black Sea coast. In summer up to seven flights go each day. If you have longer to spare, or are more conscious of your budget, several private firms run daily buses between the capital's international bus station and Varna until about 22.30. Buses also go directly to some of the other resorts. The journey takes over six hours and costs around 20 leva. For the same price you can take the train, which takes a couple of hours longer.

From Bourgas airport, the number 15 bus goes to Garov Ploshtad, which is also where trains and inter-city buses drop off. From there much of the accommodation is a short walk away. Hire cars are available too.

Varna airport is also served by bus, the 409, which goes on to Golden Sands, and you can also pick up a rental car from one of several outlets at the airport.

COMMUNICATIONS

Phones

Mobile coverage is generally good – and constantly improving – in Bulgaria, and you should have little trouble making and receiving calls and text messages in your resort, although coverage may be patchier in mountain areas. Public telephones are fairly plentiful too – you can pick

TELEPHONING BULGARIA

To call Bulgaria from overseas, dial the codes listed below followed
by the local number, but remember to drop the first 0 from the
Bulgarian number.

From the UK 00 359
From the US and Canada 011 359
From Australia and New Zealand 00 11 359
From South Africa 090 359

TELEPHONING ABROAD

To make a call abroad from Bulgaria, dial the codes listed below
followed by the local number, again minus the initial 0.

The UK 00 44
The US and Canada 00 1
Australia 00 61
New Zealand 00 64
South Africa 00 27

up a phonecard in your hotel, post office or some public buildings. Failing
that, post offices often have special rooms where you can go to make a
call. As in most countries, calls made from your hotel are likely to be
extortionately priced and are best avoided.

Post

Post offices are usually open weekdays, and sometimes Saturdays, from
08.30–17.30. Letters can take a week and a half to reach the UK and
Western Europe, and double that to get to the US. Buy stamps, which are
fairly inexpensive, from the post office.

CUSTOMS

In Bulgaria, nodding your head means no and shaking it indicates a yes,
which can be very confusing for visitors! However, many Bulgarians are
aware of this, and when talking to visitors try to adapt. Waving tends to

◔ *A traditional gaida (bagpipe) player*

mean the person wants you to approach them, rather than seeing you off. Wedding rings are also worn vice versa, on the right hand.

If you have the chance to socialise with the local people, be sure to clink your glass with every person and look them in the eye when toasting. Not to make eye contact is considered rude. And if you give a Bulgarian flowers, it should be an odd number. An even number of flowers is traditional at funerals, so it is considered inauspicious to give an even number on a happy occasion.

By law, you are required to carry ID at all times, so it's better to take your passport, or a photocopy of it, with you when you leave the hotel, in the unlikely event that you come into contact with the authorities.

DRESS CODES

Bulgarian society is a little more conservative than most visitors may be used to, but there is nothing like the restrictions on dress that apply in neighbouring Turkey. Some of the more formal hotel restaurants used to expect men to wear long trousers to dinner, but generally the resorts on the coast are now relaxed and fully geared up to suit their visitors' tastes and preferences.

While it used to be illegal, these days you shouldn't encounter any problems if you sunbathe topless, although it is better to find a secluded spot on the beach if possible. Some beaches also have special areas for nude bathing.

ELECTRICITY

The system here requires the common continental European two-pin plugs. You can pick up an adaptor from the airport on your way out. The supply is 220 volts, so UK appliances should work fine.

> **EMERGENCY NUMBERS**
> **Medical** 150
> **Fire** 160
> **Police** 166

EMERGENCIES

Should you fall ill and require medical attention, your best bet is to find your nearest health centre. If you are in your hotel, ask at reception for advice and assistance. If the problem is very serious, phone an ambulance or go straight to hospital. The main hospital on the Black Sea coast is Varna City Hospital ⓐ Saborna 40 ⓣ 052 22 30 41.

If you need the police, call the emergency number directly or ask your hotel receptionist to do so for you. Should you need the assistance of the embassy, the nearest one is in Sofia.

Embassies & consulates
Australia ⓣ 02 946 1334
Canada ⓣ 02 969 9710
South Africa ⓣ 02 981 6682
UK ⓣ 02 933 9222
US ⓣ 02 937 5100

GETTING AROUND

The best way of getting around depends on your plans. Most resorts, with the possible exception of Sunny Beach, can easily be covered on foot. The main attractions, restaurant and entertainment districts and beaches are typically within walking distance of each other and the town centres often have pedestrianised areas. Sunny Beach is more spread out than the other resorts, but there is a bus service, and in any case the beach and a selection of clubs, restaurants and shops should all be within easy reach of your hotel.

EMERGENCY PHRASES

Help!	Помощ!	*Pomosht!*
Fire!	Пожар!	*Pozhar!*
Stop!	Стоп!/Спри!	*Stop!/Spri!*

However, if you intend to see several of the towns on the coast, you are better off with a vehicle. Driving is the most convenient way to see all that Bulgaria's Black Sea coast has to offer, especially as some of the more interesting natural sites are difficult, if not impossible, to reach on public transport. You can hire a car at the airport, or ask at your hotel reception.

Car hire

Most major points, including the airports and larger cities, have car hire outlets, and the top international rental firms are represented here. Your hotel should also be able to help you arrange a vehicle. Hiring a car in Bulgaria is not cheap, and you should expect to pay well over 100 leva per day. Prices can be lower if you book in advance or through your travel agent, or if you go to a local firm rather than a big-name international company. However, expect the quality of the vehicle to reflect the price.

Another option for non-drivers, or anyone who is not confident getting behind the wheel in a foreign country, is to hire a car with a driver. This service is provided by car hire companies, or you could try approaching a taxi driver and negotiating with him directly.

Public transport

The Black Sea coast's more remote highlights tend to be difficult to reach by public transport, but travelling between towns under your own steam is possible with some advance planning. Trains will take you into Varna or Bourgas, but once on the coast there is no rail service and you will have to go by road transport.

Varna is the main public transport hub on the coast, and 60 different bus services leave from the town, many of which go up and down the coast to the other resorts. The main stop is in front of the cathedral. For enquiries, call ✆ 052 44 83 49. Outside Varna, the resorts usually post the bus destinations and departure times on the windows of the bus station ticket office. Private minibuses supplement the official buses.

For a more scenic ride, you can take a boat to Balchik, Sunny Beach, Nessebar or Bourgas, and some boat trips are also available between the other resorts. You will often see the details posted on a sign at the departure point on the beach.

Bear in mind that tourist transport is a magnet for pickpockets, so take the usual precautions.

DRIVING RULES & CONDITIONS

Like the rest of mainland Europe, cars drive on the right-hand side of the road. The speed limit for cars is 50 kph (30 mph) inside the towns, 90 kph (55 mph) outside and 120 kph (75 mph) on the highway. Your driving licence from home will suffice, although if you do have an international one, it's worth bringing it. Wearing a seatbelt is mandatory, and you can only use your mobile phone while driving if you have a hands-free set. If you're spotted infringing either of these laws, or speeding, you are liable for an on-the-spot fine.

Road conditions vary considerably. Some of the resorts are small and hilly, and as a result the roads may be narrow and steep, and badly parked cars in the busier towns can make turning, parking and negotiating some bends fairly tricky. On main highways between the larger towns, road surfaces are as you would expect at home and a central reservation is often in place. However, some of the minor roads are of poorer quality, with uneven surfaces and potholes. Also on these lesser-used routes, the road can sometimes narrow to less than two car widths, and you will be obliged to go off road to pass oncoming vehicles.

Street signs too can be confusing. At times absent entirely, at times only in the Cyrillic alphabet, and at times contradictory, they cannot be relied upon – and anyone intending to do a lot of driving is advised to invest in a detailed map of the region and take their cues mainly from that.

Another good idea is to avoid driving at night where possible. In parts the coast road that runs between the resorts is not lit, and with many bends to contend with, the journey can be fraught. Stick to driving in the daylight hours to avoid the worry.

HEALTH, SAFETY & CRIME

Bulgarian food and drink are unlikely to pose any problems during your stay. The tap water is safe to drink, but most tourists prefer bottled mineral water because it costs so little. While standards of restaurant hygiene are usually exemplary, if you go off the beaten track use your judgement.

The UK has a reciprocal arrangement with Bulgaria, under which medical treatment is provided free of charge, as long as you can show your passport and your European Health Insurance Card (EHIC). You will have to pay for any medicine, however. The British Embassy does not provide a list of English-speaking doctors – it's best to ask your hotel receptionist to help you if you need it.

Tourists are unlikely to encounter any serious trouble. The country has been struggling to get its organised crime under control, but out in the resorts there is little outward evidence of this. Prostitution can be a problem, particularly around certain discos and clubs in the main resorts, and the women sometimes collude with groups of thieves. Prostitutes also sometimes solicit in the clubs themselves. Though they will generally leave couples and families alone, they may hassle lone males or groups of men.

Bulgarian police are fairly easy to spot due to their military-style uniforms. The country has greatly cleaned up its act and is doing its best to tackle its corruption. That said, you may find the local police less helpful than you would expect, and if you're reporting a theft, for example, a small bribe can help to oil the wheels. While a few years ago foreign motorists feared being stopped and fined, now the traffic police take little interest in tourists unless they are overtly flouting the traffic laws.

Bulgaria's Black Sea coast feels a safe region for a foreigner to travel in, but do bear in mind that it is a poor country and that there will always be people who see tourists as rich, easy targets. Take all the usual precautions that you would when travelling abroad. Don't advertise your valuables, keep your cash in a safe place, and try not to leave expensive items in your hotel room unless you feel very comfortable with the security level.

MEDIA

The larger resorts are very in tune with their guests' tastes, and British, German and French newspapers – in particular tabloids – are often on sale in the lobbies of the more upmarket hotels, usually a couple of days out of date. The typical international news magazines are also on sale in some petrol stations and kiosks.

◓ Both foreign and local newspapers are available

American films are common on Bulgarian TV channels, sometimes with subtitles and at other times dubbed. Your hotel is likely to have a cable package, which should include CNN and BBC World at the least, plus other standards like the Discovery Channel, Animal Planet, Euronews, Eurosport and MTV.

OPENING HOURS

Banks are usually open from 09.00 to 16.00, Monday to Friday. Museums' working hours vary, but tend to be from 09.00 to 17.00 or 18.00 in the busier resorts. In smaller towns, museums often close for lunch at around 12.00 or 12.30 and reopen half an hour or an hour later. The smallest museums often keep quite erratic hours, and it can be a case of knocking on the door and hoping for the best. Most display their opening hours on or near the front door, but this is no guarantee that they stick to them. Shops and stores are generally open from 10.00 to 20.00, Monday to Friday, and from 10.00 to 14.00 on Saturday. In the main tourist resorts, though, you may also find some stores open later and also on Sunday.

RELIGION

Bulgaria is a Christian country, with the vast majority of the people counting themselves as belonging to the Bulgarian Orthodox faith. Icons are common, in both museums and shops, and the country celebrates frequent saints' days. There is also a significant minority of Muslims, around 12 per cent. However, while the local people may seem devout in the celebration of their festivals and iconography, Bulgaria is not a place where religious standards are imposed on outsiders. Along the Black Sea coast in particular, foreign tastes are catered for and foreign ways generally respected. Though they may not choose to follow suit, Bulgarians are unlikely to have any problem with tourists who sunbathe topless or have a glass or two too many of the local red wine or spirits!

TIME DIFFERENCES

Bulgaria is two hours ahead of the UK and one hour ahead of Western Europe. It is ten hours in front of the West Coast US and seven ahead of the East Coast. It is nine hours behind New Zealand time, five hours behind West Coast Australia and seven behind East Coast Australia. Clocks change on the last Sundays in March and October.

TIPPING

Tipping was not customary in Bulgaria, but the tourist influx seems to have changed that. Now 10 to 12 per cent is common for waiters and waitresses, and it's normal to leave a small something for the cleaners and doormen in your hotel. Taxi drivers do not usually expect a tip.

TOILETS

Toilets on the Black Sea coast run the gamut from squat toilets – mercifully the exception rather than the rule – to designer conveniences with the end of the loo paper folded neatly into a point. In general the kind of establishment you are in should give you a clue. Some of the cheaper restaurants charge for the use of their toilet, even if you are a customer, and it's an idea to keep some small change on you in the smaller resorts just in case. You are unlikely to come across anything too bad, but in the more out-of-the-way places toilets and bathrooms may look a little shabbier than you are used to. When you're on the road, stick to the facilities in the chain petrol stations, which should all be fine.

TRAVELLERS WITH DISABILITIES

Bulgaria is not the easiest country in which to travel if you have a disability. Its infrastructure has been improving rapidly over recent years, and some of the larger, higher-ranked hotels now have reliable lifts and ramps, but this is not the norm and cannot be assumed. You should call and check with the hotel before booking. The Holiday Care site provides some information for people with disabilities planning a holiday. While Bulgaria does not feature in the list of countries about which they have special recommendations, they should be able to give you more general advice about planning your trip. ❶ 0845 124 9971
Ⓦ www.holidaycare.org.uk Ⓔ info@tourismforall.org.uk

SPOT THE BEST BEACHES

Now we help you to get more from your holiday before you've even unpacked your sun cream. Each great pocket guide covers everything your chosen resort has to offer, meaning you'll have so much more to tell the folks back home. We've included everything from the best bars, clubs and restaurants to family-friendly attractions and of course all of those sun-drenched beaches.

HOTSPOTS
ALGARVE

HOTSPOTS
MOROCCO

Titles in the series include:
Algarve, Bulgaria, Corfu, Corsica, Costa Blanca, Costa Brava & Costa Dorada, Costa del Sol & Costa de Almeria, Côte D'Azur, Crete, Croatia, Cuba, Cyprus, Dominican Republic, Egypt, Fuerteventura, Gran Canaria, Guernsey, Ibiza, Ionian Islands, Jersey, Lanzarote, Mallorca, Malta, Menorca, Mexico, Morocco, Orlando, Rhodes & Kos, Tenerife, Tunisia and Turkey.

Available from all good bookshops, your local Thomas Cook travel store or browse and buy on-line at www.thomascookpublishing.com

Thomas Cook Publishing

ACKNOWLEDGEMENTS

The publishers would like to thank the following individuals and organisations for providing their copyright photographs for this book: Fotolia/Ecoview page 67; Christopher Hurry page 83; Pictures Colour Library pages 13, 105; StockaPhoto/Nikolay Dimitrov page 80; World Pictures pages 1, 5, 8, 10, 16, 21, 25, 28, 30, 34, 36, 42, 44, 48, 50, 63, 72, 85, 107, 109, 112, 116, 122; all the rest, Vasile Szakacs.

Copy editor: Penny Isaac
Proofreader: Ian Faulkner

Send your thoughts to
books@thomascook.com

- Found a beach bar, peaceful stretch of sand or must-see sight that we don't feature?

- Like to tip us off about any information that needs a little updating?

- Want to tell us what you love about this handy little guidebook and more importantly how we can make it even handier?

Then here's your chance to tell all! Send us ideas, discoveries and recommendations today and then look out for your valuable input in the next edition of this title. And, as an extra 'thank you' from Thomas Cook Publishing, you'll be automatically entered into our exciting prize draw.

Send an email to the above address or write to:
HotSpots Project Editor, Thomas Cook Publishing, PO Box 227, Unit 18, Coningsby Road, Peterborough PE3 8SB, UK